# Honestly Speaking

# Invitation One: To Humble Curiosity

Psalm 138:6
"Though the Lord is great, He cares for the humble, but He keeps His distance from the proud."
Let's start here—not with answers, not with effort, not with resolve.
Let's simply start with honest humility and curiosity, without judgment.
I've been realizing something over the last year, and I want to say it out loud, as plainly as I can: a lot of areas of my life have drifted out of balance, and not because they were bad things.
Honestly, most of them were good things, meaningful things, and life-giving things—at least at first. But when too much weight gathers on one side, even good things start to pull harder than they should.
Psalm 138 reminds me that God is great—and that He comes close to humility.
It does not say He comes close to the perfectly polished ones that others perceive to have it all together, close to competence, or close to the version of us that looks steady and capable.
God comes close to HUMILITY.
That should compel us to absolute truth and openness. And that's the posture I want to invite you into with me. Let's delve into the depths, together, with curiosity, leaving judgment behind.
Think of a scale for a moment—the kind with two sides. When everything is reasonably balanced, the whole thing functions the way it's meant to. But when one side keeps collecting weight—responsibility, expectations, roles, strengths, coping strategies—the other side lifts higher and higher.

Eventually, the things we need most are still there... but they're out of reach.

Not because they disappeared, not because we failed, but because the balance shifted.

That's what this last season has felt like for me. There were things I needed—rest, clarity, deeper healing, grace for myself, unhurried joy—but I couldn't quite grab hold of them.

Not because I didn't want to, but because there was so much weight pressing down on the other side of the scale that I couldn't lower myself enough to reach what I needed.

And here's where humility quietly enters.

Humility isn't admitting we've messed everything up. It's admitting when something is heavier than it should be.

Psalm 138 doesn't say God keeps His distance from the broken or the confused. It says He keeps His distance from the proud—the version of us that insists on holding everything together, managing the weight, compensating endlessly, never stopping long enough to ask whether things still belong where they are.

I started noticing that some of my greatest strengths—things God truly has gifted me with—had slowly become tools for keeping life under control.

They helped me stay productive. They helped me stay functional. They helped me keep moving.

But they also kept me from slowing down long enough to look honestly at what I had set aside. This was not because I didn't care. This was because I was out of balance. And when you're out of balance, even curiosity feels like a luxury.

So this book—this path we're stepping onto together—isn't about piling more weight onto the scale.

It's about redistributing the weight.

It's about letting things return to where they actually belong. Some weight needs to come off the side we've been leaning on too heavily. Some weight needs to be acknowledged instead of ignored. Some weight turns out not to be weight at all—just fear we've been carrying unnecessarily.

And Psalm 138 keeps whispering through all of it: God comes close here—in this humble posture, and in this honest curiosity.
It's not when we've sorted everything out. It's not when we've labeled things neatly as good or bad, strength or weakness. But it's when we're willing to look at all of it— with curiosity instead of judgment.
That's the invitation today.
No shame. Nothing off-limits. Nothing rushed.

Just the gentle decision to say, "I want to bring my life back into balance—not so I can avoid the deeper places, but so I finally have the reach to go there."
God is not threatened by what you'll find when you start plumbing the depths. He's not waiting for you to fix it before He comes near. According to Psalm 138, He's already leaning in—drawn by humility, by truth, by your willingness to stop pretending that imbalance is sustainable.
So, let's sit here together for a moment and see it all.
Let's look at the scale without flinching. Let's stay curious. This is how light begins to form. This is how freedom becomes possible. And this is where the path starts—not with pressure, but with grace.

# Questions to Prayerfully Ponder

Where in my life has "too much weight" quietly collected —even from good things—and what is one small, honest step I can take today to begin redistributing that weight so I can reach what I truly need?
What good thing have I been leaning on so heavily that it's keeping me from balance—and am I willing to loosen my grip so God can restore what belongs where?

## Prayer

God, I admit that I have been carrying good things as though they were meant to hold me up. Responsibilities, strengths, callings, even gifts— I've let them bear more weight than they were ever designed to carry.
Today, I release my grip.
Not because these things are wrong, but because I don't want them ruling the balance of my life. I don't want control disguised as faith, or productivity mistaken for trust.
Show me where the weight has gathered. Reveal what I've been managing instead of surrendering. And give me the courage to loosen my hands even when I don't yet know what will replace the strain.
I choose humility over control. Truth over appearance. Balance over striving.
Take what is good but heavy, and place it where it belongs. Free my reach for what I truly need— rest, clarity, joy, and the quiet strength that comes from You alone.
I trust You with the redistribution. I trust You with the unknown. And I trust that what I release today will make room for a freedom I cannot manufacture on my own.
Amen

# Invitation Two: To Uncover the Roots

Hebrews 4:13
"Nothing in all creation is hidden from God. Everything is naked and exposed before His eyes, and He is the one to whom we are accountable."
There's something both comforting and unsettling about this verse. Comforting, because nothing about us surprises God. Unsettling, because nothing is actually hidden. Hebrews doesn't say God will eventually see everything. It says He already does.
And yet—if I'm honest—I still bury things. Not because I'm trying to deceive God. But because I don't always know what to do with what I find inside myself.
Sometimes I bury things out of fear. Sometimes out of shame. Sometimes out of confusion. And sometimes simply because I don't yet have language for what I'm carrying.
So I set it aside. I move on. I tell myself it's dealt with. But buried doesn't mean gone.
I learned that once in a very literal way. We were burning a controlled fire in a cleared area, working to remove vegetation.
When we were finished, we did everything right—we saturated the ground with water, soaked the surface thoroughly, checked and rechecked. There was no smoke, no heat, no sign of anything still burning. Everyone left confident it was fully extinguished.
Hours later, we discovered something none of us had seen. Tree roots ran deep beneath the surface of the soil—far below where the water had reached. And those roots had quietly fed the fire. What looked cold and finished on the surface was still burning underneath.
That underground fire had the potential to cause real damage if it hadn't been discovered and addressed.

That image has stayed with me. Because there are times in my life when I've assumed something was extinguished— an old wound, a fear, a disappointment, a survival habit— only to realize later that it was still burning quietly beneath the surface.
Not loudly.
Not dramatically.
Just steadily.
Feeding other reactions.
Influencing decisions.
Touching areas of my life I never would have connected back to that buried place.
Hebrews 4:13 gently reminds me that God sees those roots. Not with accusation. Not with impatience. But with clarity. And that's where the invitation lies. God already sees what's buried.
The question isn't whether He knows—it's whether I'm willing to look, too. Whether I'm willing to drag my fears into the light and see them for what they really are, instead of letting them quietly run the show.
This kind of exposure isn't about punishment. It's about purification. When I come to God asking for forgiveness, direction, clarity, reassurance, wisdom—something begins to happen. My thoughts are revealed. My motivations become clearer.
The stories I've been telling myself get gently tested by truth. And truth, when handled by a loving God, doesn't destroy. It refines.
Light and life are inseparable. God is the source of both. But here's something I'm learning: light isn't found only above, in the obvious, polished, elevated places. Sometimes light is found below. Sometimes it's hidden in the very places we avoid—beneath the soil, wrapped around old roots, in places we assumed were cold and harmless.

And when we're brave enough to look there, we don't just discover darkness. We often discover fire—energy, passion, intensity—that was never meant to harm us, but was never meant to remain hidden either. When those roots are exposed and surrendered, God can do something astonishing.

He can take what was silently harming us and reframe it. Contain it. Transform it. What once threatened destruction can become warmth. Guidance. Light. Not just for us—but for others as well. Because when God's light is allowed to remain exposed in us, people don't just experience us. They experience Him through the ordinary spaces of our lives.

Through our presence.

Our steadiness.

Our compassion.

Our freedom.

Most of them will never know the roots you dug up. They'll just know the light feels real and it feels good. It feels like something they have been longing for. And that's why this is worth it.

So consider this your permission slip. Permission to go where most people avoid. Permission to look beneath the surface. Permission to dig—not recklessly, but prayerfully. Permission to believe that nothing you uncover is wasted in God's hands. The buried places don't disappear on their own. But they don't have to remain hidden, either.

So today, let's go down. On purpose. With intention. Not to dwell in darkness—but to let light reach places it's been waiting to transform all along.

# Questions to Prayerfully Consider

What is one place in my life that I've assumed was "extinguished," but may still be quietly influencing my thoughts, reactions, or decisions—and what might happen if I invited God to help me gently uncover the root beneath it?
What buried fear, wound, or unfinished story might still be feeding my life beneath the surface—and am I willing, today, to let God bring light to it instead of continuing to manage its effects?

## Prayer

God, You already see what's hidden in me—
not with judgment, but with love.
So today, I stop managing the buried places
and place them gently into Your hands.
The fears I learned to live with.
The wounds I learned to protect.
The fire still burning beneath the surface.
I trust You to purify what was harming me
and to transform it into light that gives life.
Where there was quiet damage, bring healing.
Where there was heaviness, bring freedom.
Where there was fear, bring clarity and peace.
I release what no longer belongs underground.
And as Your light reaches these places,
I receive the joy and lightness that follow surrender.
Thank You for the freedom that comes
not from hiding—but from being fully seen and held.
Amen

# Invitation Three: To Be Known

Psalm 139:23–24
"Search me, God, and know my heart;
test me and know my anxious thoughts.
See if there is any offensive way in me,
and lead me in the way everlasting."
God already knows what my heart contains.
He already knows the thoughts I construct, the fears I
avoid, and the things I run to when I feel anxious—
especially the ones that promise comfort but offer very
little life.
And still, this prayer invites Him to search me.
I think that's because there's a difference between being
willing to go deep and being willing to be known.
Most of us don't really resist growth. We're open to the idea
of becoming healthier, freer, more whole. What's much
harder is vulnerability—the kind that allows ourselves to be
seen clearly. Truly known. Especially in the places we're not
proud of, the places that feel darker, messier, or more
fragile.
Because being known carries risk.
When I'm exposed or vulnerable with another person,
there's often a question hovering just beneath the surface:
Can they be trusted with this?
Will they walk with me toward freedom and joy?
Or will they quietly store this away—something to be used
later, to control, influence, or wound me if it ever becomes
convenient?
Those fears don't come from nowhere.
And that's why Psalm 139 matters so much.
This prayer isn't asking God to fix anything first.
It's asking Him to search.
That word requires immense trust.
Searching means slowing down. Letting the noise settle.

Removing the distractions and the busyness that keep us focused on what's shallow, obvious, or easier to manage. It means allowing ourselves to notice not just what we prefer to look at, but what's actually there.
When we slow down enough, familiar reactions begin to surface.
The places our thoughts go automatically when we're tired, hungry, pressured, afraid, or unsure.
The responses that feel instinctive—so natural we rarely question them.
Imbalance doesn't usually announce itself loudly.
It shows up quietly, through patterns.
Maybe it's the way I hurry when I feel uncomfortable.
Or the way I explain instead of listening.
Maybe it's the way I retreat when something feels too vulnerable.
Or the way I take responsibility for things that were never mine to carry.
Many of these patterns once served a purpose. They protected us. They helped us survive. They made life manageable when we didn't yet have better tools.
Psalm 139 invites us to let God look at those patterns with us—not to shame us for having them, but to help us understand why they formed, and whether they still belong.
Because what once protected us can eventually limit us. And what once helped us cope can quietly begin to cost us freedom.
When I pray, "Search me," I'm not asking God to expose me to embarrassment or condemnation. I'm asking Him to help me see myself clearly—with the same honesty and care He already has.
That kind of awareness is holy work.
It requires humility.
And it requires trust.

God is the one who can be trusted without reservation. He doesn't reveal in order to harm. He reveals in order to lead —"in the way everlasting." That phrase matters.
God isn't interested in short-term fixes or surface behavior. He's interested in the kind of freedom that lasts. The kind that reshapes not just what we do, but why we do it. How we think. How we respond. How we relate.
So today, ask Him to search you.
Ask Him to show you what you need to see.
Notice what surfaces when you're stressed.
Notice what you avoid when things feel uncertain.
Notice what you reach for instinctively to feel safe, capable, accepted, or in control.
Invite God to take those once-valuable tendencies and bring them into the light.
Because when He leads, it isn't harsh.
It's steady.
And it is kind.
He is kind.
This is how balance begins to form.
This is how exposure becomes understanding.
This is how transformation starts.

Let Him show you what He sees.
Let Him show you how He sees you.
Let Him show you how deeply He adores you.
And trust Him to put His arm around you and walk you—
gently, faithfully—into healing and freedom.
For me, when I feel unsure or afraid, I become hyper-
busy. If I can't fix the problem itself, I'll fix something—
anything—in the physical world around me.
Think of a jar of water.
If it's filled with dirt and impurities, but the jar is still,
everything settles at the bottom. From the surface, it may
look clear enough. You might even pour yourself a drink,
unaware that what's hidden is still affecting you.
But shake the jar—rattle it even slightly—and suddenly the
contents are obvious. The water clouds. You can't ignore
what's there anymore. You may not know exactly what
each impurity is, but you know enough to stop and say, "I
shouldn't consume this until it's been purified."
Wouldn't it be wiser to purify the water
than to spend your life making sure the jar never gets
bumped?
God's searching is not meant to make us anxious.
It's meant to make us whole.
Let Him search.
Let Him clarify.
Let Him purify.
And trust that what He reveals, He also heals.

## Reflective Question

What pattern do I rely on most when I feel anxious or uncertain—and what might God want to show me about why I reach for it, and whether it still belongs in my life today?

## Prayer

God, You already know me completely,
and still You invite me to be seen.
So today, I stop hiding behind busyness, explanations,
or the patterns I've learned to rely on.
I invite You to search me—not to expose me to harm,
but to lead me into freedom.
Show me what I reach for when I feel anxious or unsure.
Help me understand what once protected me
and what no longer needs to remain.
Give me courage to release what has outlived its purpose
and trust You with what feels vulnerable.
Thank You that Your searching is gentle,
Your truth is kind,
and Your guidance is steady.
Lead me in the way everlasting—
not just changing what I do,
but healing what drives me to do it.
I place myself in Your care,
fully known, deeply loved,
and willing to be led.
Amen

# Invitation Four: To Be Tenderly Held

Deuteronomy 31:8
"It is the Lord who goes before you;
He will be with you.
He will not fail you or abandon you.
Do not fear or be dismayed."
This was a promise God gave to a people He had already
proven Himself to.
These were the people He delivered out of bondage.
The people He walked with through uncertainty.
The people He was leading—not just away from
something painful, but into freedom and promise.
That matters to me.
Because it tells me something essential about His
character.
God didn't make this promise casually, and He didn't make
it once. He made it after showing His faithfulness again
and again—when His people were afraid, tired, unsure, and
standing on unfamiliar ground. And I'm certain His
character hasn't changed. His faithfulness hasn't
diminished. His care hasn't weakened.
In my own life, He has never failed me.
Not once.
He doesn't always hurry.
He doesn't always explain Himself on my timeline.
But He has always remained faithful.
Always.
And more often than not, He has been far more than I
expected—even considering our long, shared history
together.
That faithfulness isn't just reassuring to me.
It's foundational.
It's what I've built my life on.
And still... I need to be honest.
What frustrates me most isn't that fear shows up
sometimes—it's that I know better.

We have an amazing track record. An unbroken history of care and provision. I know His faithfulness. I know His strong, tender care for me. I've watched Him show up again and again in ways I never could have orchestrated myself.

And yet, there are moments—sometimes entire days—when things come at me from multiple directions, and the what-ifs begin swirling through my thoughts. Suddenly, I feel entirely alone.

Even though I know He goes before me and prepares the way.

Even though I know He goes behind me to protect me.

Even though I know He walks beside me.

Even though I know I am surrounded by His very being.

I know all of that.

So I catch myself thinking, Why am I feeling this way? I shouldn't feel anxious. I shouldn't feel afraid. I shouldn't feel like I'm carrying everything by myself. I shouldn't feel so overwhelmed.

And that frustration turns inward.

But I'm learning that knowing truth in my head doesn't mean my heart and body have fully learned how to rest in it yet.

There's something in me that's still adjusting.

Maybe it's learning what it means to be truly alone in a way I never was before. Maybe it's something that never had to develop earlier in my life because I always lived under the strong covering of my father, and then my husband.

Maybe it's grief finding its voice in unfamiliar ways.

I don't know exactly what it is.

And I'm realizing I don't actually need to know where it came from as much as I need to know what to do with it.

So I crawl up into God's lap and ask Him honestly, "What do I do with this?"
Not with shame.
Not with self-correction.
But with trust.
Because I want to be faithful to Him the way He has always been faithful to me. I want to take the thing that overwhelms me—the racing thoughts, the spiraling what-ifs, the moments where I'm brought to tears—and place it into His hands.
Not so it disappears.
But so He can transform it.
And that's where an image keeps coming back to me.
I think about my babies when they were small—those nighttime hours when the world was quiet and dark, and the very best thing for them was to be full, warm, and laid down in their crib, drifting into peaceful sleep.
There came an age when that wasn't quite enough. They needed reassurance. They needed to know that I—or their daddy—was there.
And when they needed that, we didn't turn on the lights or pick them up or say a word. We would simply lay a gentle hand on their back. Just enough weight for them to feel our presence. Just enough to reassure them that they were not alone.
As long as they felt that, they would fall asleep—confident, comfortable, and at peace.
Once they were asleep, we would quietly remove our hand and go back to our own bed. But taking our hand away didn't mean we left them. We were still there. Still listening. Still protecting. Still providing.
We could hear their breathing.
We whispered with gratitude about how beautiful they were.
We smiled when they smacked their little lips or hiccupped in their sleep.
Their very existence brought us joy.

They had no idea how closely they were being watched.
How deeply they were adored.
And I realize—that's how God is with me.
When I don't feel His hand, He hasn't withdrawn His care.
When I feel alone in the quiet, He is still there—watching,
protecting, providing, delighting.
For my growth.
For my development.
For my good.
He allows this season of quiet not as abandonment, but as
purpose.
And I get to choose what I do with it.
I can waste it—worrying, fretting, spiraling through the
what-ifs, convincing myself I'm alone when I know I'm not.
Or I can rest—trusting that He has not gone anywhere, that
His presence is steady even when it isn't tangible, and that
His faithfulness hasn't taken a single step back.
Deuteronomy 31:8 isn't just a comfort.
It's a companion.
He goes before me.
He stays with me.
He does not fail me.
And He does not abandon me.
Even here.
Especially here.
And maybe—just maybe—this quiet is not something to
fear, but something to receive.

## Questions to prayerfully consider

When I feel most alone or overwhelmed, what do I
instinctively do to reassure myself—and what might
change if I allowed myself to rest in the quiet truth that
God is still present, watching over me with care I don't
have to feel in order to trust?
Where have I mistaken God's quietness for absence—and
am I willing today to trust that His unseen presence is still
holding me?

## PRAYER

God, I'm not pretending to be brave right now. There are
moments when the quiet scares me, when the weight feels
heavier than I expected, and when trust feels costly.
So I'm telling You the truth.
I feel alone sometimes—even though I know I'm not. I feel
overwhelmed—even though I know You go before me. I
feel afraid—even though I know Your faithfulness by heart.
And still... I choose You.
I choose to trust You when my feelings lag behind my faith.
I choose to believe that Your silence is not absence, that
Your unseen presence is still holding me steady.

I bring You my fear without dressing it up. I bring You my
exhaustion without apology. I bring You the what-ifs that
swirl when I'm tired and unsure.
I cannot carry all of this alone—and I was never meant to.
So I place myself fully in Your care. Not because I feel
ready, but because You are faithful. Not because I
understand the way forward, but because You already do.
Hold me when I can't hold myself. Reassure me when I
forget. Stay near when I don't feel brave enough to ask.
I trust You—not because this is easy, but because You have
never, ever let me down.
I rest in You now. Fully known. Deeply loved. And safe.
Amen

# Invitation Five: To Remember I Am Not the Actual Source

Deuteronomy 8:17–18 (Easy English)
"You must never say to yourself, 'I've got all these valuable things because I am strong and clever.'
Instead, you must always remember the Lord your God.
He is the one who gives you the strength to get good things.
He does that to show that his covenant still has authority today—
the covenant he promised to your ancestors."
This verse doesn't scold me.
It steadies me.
God wasn't speaking to people who had done nothing. He was speaking to people who had worked, endured, gathered, built. People who understood effort and responsibility. And He wasn't saying, "Don't work." He was saying, "Don't forget where the strength comes from."
When I read this now, it lands differently than it would have earlier in my life.
I'm fifty-eight years old. I've been self-employed my entire adult life. I didn't build a traditional retirement. There was no automatic safety net quietly growing in the background.
If income came in, it was because I worked for it. If it didn't, it wasn't there.
That reality grows louder with age.
I'm aware there will come a day when I either can't, shouldn't, or simply don't want to keep working at the same pace just to cover living expenses, let alone the joys and necessities of life. And as a widow, I know something very plainly: if I don't produce the income, it won't magically appear.

So yes—there is wisdom in planning.
There is wisdom in producing.
There is wisdom in building income streams that don't require constant physical output.
God is not offended by diligence.
But there is a line between diligence and striving.
And I've been standing close enough to that line to notice it.
Striving feels urgent.
Diligence feels anchored.
As I've been pondering this, I've realized the place I need to go deeper isn't actually about money at all. It's about fear.
What is it, really, that I'm afraid of when I think about savings running out?
What is it about income shrinking, or expenses growing, that makes my chest tighten?
What am I imagining will happen if I can't cover every future base—especially the ones I don't even know yet?
What if the savings does run out?
What if I'm unable to work more, and life still asks for more from me?
Those questions reveal something deeper than numbers.
They reveal a fear of lack. A fear of vulnerability. A fear of being exposed without a safety net I can control.
And that's where I realize I don't need better spreadsheets as much as I need deeper honesty.
This is another place where I crawl up into God's lap and ask, "What is this?"
Not How do I fix it?

But What am I really afraid of?
And then, What do I do with this when I find it?
Because striving to cover every possible future scenario
isn't just exhausting—it's an attempt to be my own source.
That's where the image of light keeps coming back to me.
If I walk into a dark space carrying my own light, it's easy
to think I'm the one illuminating it. But I'm not the source.
Whatever light I'm holding has to be powered by
something else—and if I stop feeding it, it goes dark.
So I keep striving.
Keep managing.
Keep exhausting myself trying to sustain what I was never
meant to sustain.
God, on the other hand, is light.
He doesn't have to go to a source to produce it.
He doesn't have to strive to keep it going.
He is clothed in light. It flows from who He is.
So when I start fearing lack—when I feel compelled to
overwork, overplan, overcontrol—this verse gently brings
me back to truth: I am not the source.
And that isn't failure.
It's freedom.
God gives me the power to get wealth—not so I can wear
myself out proving I'm capable, but so I can work with
Him, trusting that the source never runs dry.
My part is diligence.
His part is provision.
My part is tending the light.
His part is being the light.

When I forget that, I don't just lose peace—I lose perspective. I miss the beauty of what's right in front of me because I'm straining toward a future I can't fully see or control anyway.

So I want to take this fear—this fear of lack, of running out, of not being enough—and place it in God's hands. I want Him to show me what's underneath it, and then transform it into something purposeful. Something strong. Something that doesn't just steady me, but blesses the people around me.

I don't want to walk through life braced for scarcity when I'm already being cared for.

I want to be diligent, yes—but not fearful.

Wise—but not frantic.

Active—but not exhausted.

Because God has never failed me.

And He is not starting now.

## Reflective Question

When I worry about money, provision, or the future, what am I truly afraid of losing—and what does that fear reveal about where I'm still trying to be my own source?

## Prayer

Father, I come to You with the fear beneath my striving.

The fear of running out.

The fear of not having enough.

The fear of being responsible for what I was never meant to supply on my own.

I release that fear to You now.
I confess the ways I've tried to be my own source—
measuring, calculating, bracing, striving—
as though provision depended solely on my strength or
foresight.
You are my source.
You always have been.
Everything I have ever needed has flowed from Your care,
and everything I will need still rests safely in Your hands.
You do not grow weary.
You do not run out.
You do not forget Your children.
So today, I choose to tend my relationship with You above
all else.
I choose intimacy over anxiety.
Trust over control.
Presence over pressure.
As I draw near to You, I trust that You will continue to
provide—
wisdom when I need direction,
strength when I need endurance,
and provision in the ways only You can orchestrate.
I will do my part with diligence and faithfulness,
but I release the burden of being the source.
That belongs to You.
Thank You for being a good Father.
Thank You for caring for me completely.
Thank You that lack does not have the final word—
because You are enough.
I rest in You now.
Confident.
Provided for.
And deeply loved.
Amen

# Invitation Six: To Let Joy Take Root

## Prayer

Father,
Here we are—six days in—
standing more honest than when we began,
a little quieter, a little less defended,
a little more aware of what has been shaping us beneath the surface.
We've chosen humility over hiding.
We've allowed light to reach places we once buried.
We've invited You to search us, to know us, to lead us.
We've named our fears—of being alone, of running out, of carrying too much.
And we've remembered again that You are the source of all that sustains us.
Thank You for meeting us here with kindness.
Thank You for never shaming what You reveal.
Thank You for never withdrawing when we bring You the truth.
Thank You for welcoming us in—not because we were polished or prepared,
but because You desired us.


We ask that this work would not stay contained within us.
As You bring balance, let it steady our presence.
As You heal hidden places, let it soften our responses.
As You replace fear with trust, let it free our hands and our hearts.
Let the transformation You're doing in us
become an invitation to those around us—
not through words we force—
but through lives that feel different to be near.

May people encounter peace where there used to be
striving.
Safety where there used to be guardedness.
Light where there once was fear of lack.
Not because we have become something impressive—
but because You are faithfully, beautifully at work within
us.
Continue to lead us deeper.
Continue to shape us gently.
Continue to remind us that we belong.
And as we walk this path,
may our lives quietly say to the world:
Come and see—there is room here,
and there is a God who is good.
We trust You with what You've begun.
We trust You with what's still unfolding.
And we offer ourselves—open, willing, and grateful.
Amen

**Beneath the Surface**

If you find yourself not quite ready to move on—
if something in these last days is still stirring—
this space is for you.
You don't need to rush.
You don't need to resolve anything here.
This is simply an invitation to sit a bit closer to the fire,
to let the warmth linger,
and to notice what rises when the noise settles.

The questions below aren't meant to be answered quickly
or completely.
They're meant to be lived with—
carried into prayer, journaling, quiet walks, or long pauses.
Take the ones that resonate.
Leave the rest for another time.

## Questions to Consider

Where is my focus most often resting right now—
especially when life feels uncertain or demanding?
What is my joy currently anchored to?
Is it rooted in things, experiences, people,
accomplishments, dreams, or future outcomes?
When those things feel threatened, delayed, or
unavailable, what happens inside me?
Where do I sense God inviting my joy to be more deeply
rooted?
Do I believe God delights in my joy, or do I feel tension
around enjoying good things?
How do I currently hold the things of the world alongside
the things of the Lord?
Am I allowing space for joy in everyday delights while
keeping my heart aligned with God?
What gently brings me back into joyful alignment when I
notice myself drifting?
What practices, rhythms, or boundaries help me remain
present with God rather than striving ahead of Him?
If you'd like, you might close this time with a simple
prayer:
God, show me what lives beneath the surface—
and meet me there with Your kindness.
That alone is enough.

# Invitation Seven: To Choose Relationship Over Religion

John 14:3–6
"When everything is ready, I will come and get you, so that
you will always be with me where I am.
And you know the way to where I am going."
"No, we don't know, Lord," Thomas said. "We have no idea
where you are going, so how can we know the way?"
Jesus told him, "I am the way, the truth, and the life. No
one can come to the Father except through me."
There's something deeply telling about this exchange.
Jesus doesn't give directions.
He doesn't hand them a map.
He doesn't outline a system or a formula.
He says, "I am the way."
That tells me something important:
Knowing about God is not the same as knowing God.
We can learn everything there is to know about Him—His
nature, His character, His promises—and if that knowledge
doesn't lead us into encounter, into relationship, into
nearness, then we haven't actually met Him. We've just
agreed with information.
And agreement alone doesn't transform a life.
This is where religion quietly slips in.
Religion has value. It really does. It can point us toward
God. It can give us structure. It can help us begin. But
religion also has tentacles—and those tentacles can stretch
into every facet of our lives without us even noticing.
When that happens, something subtle shifts.
We stop crawling up into God's lap.
We stop leaning into relationship.
And instead, we begin reaching for formulas.
What can I do for Him so that He will do for me?
If I'm faithful here, will He be obligated there?
If I check the right boxes, will I stay in good standing?

And without realizing it, we make God powerless in our lives—not because He is powerless, but because we've decided we don't actually want relationship. We want predictability. Control. Assurance we can manage.
But God doesn't live inside frameworks like that.
He is living.
He is present.
He is relational.
And He will not be reduced to an exchange system.
Jesus had already done everything necessary. The spotless Lamb had already been decided. Nothing was left for us to earn.
And yet, religion keeps tempting us to act as though something still is.
As humans, we often look to people who seem to be in "good standing" with God. Their lives become billboards—examples meant to point us in the right direction. And there is value in learning from those who are walking closely with Him.
But here's the danger.
If I'm driving my grandchildren to a theme park—their hearts full of anticipation, trusting me to get them there—and I pull over at the first billboard and declare, "We've arrived," I've failed them.
I can create games at the base of that billboard.
I can hand out snacks.
I can hype the moment and call it the best day ever.
But those children have not experienced the real thing.
No matter how much I manufacture joy, I've robbed them of the actual destination.
That's what religion does when it replaces relationship.
We camp at the billboard.
We build activity there.
We call it fulfillment.
But we never actually arrive.
And I say this gently, because I know it firsthand.

I'm fifty-eight years old. I've been in relationship with God through Christ since I was twelve. And I am still—daily—unwinding the tentacles of religion from my life.
They've wound themselves through every part of me.
They're not entirely without value; they led me into relationship in the beginning. But they were never meant to be the relationship. And over time, they limited my understanding of who I am in Christ, who Christ is in me, and how God's purpose touches every detail of my life.
They affected how I responded to events.
How I interpreted hardship.
How I understood freedom and joy.
So now—today, and every day—I crawl back into God's lap.
I quiet myself.
I lean into His arms.
I stay still long enough to hear a heartbeat I know is His.
And I ask Him to show me where religion has crowded out relationship.
Where man's instruction has confused divine impartation.
Where freedom has been stifled by systems that were never meant to replace intimacy.
Jesus didn't say, "Follow these steps."
He said, "Come to the Father through me."
He is the way.
Not the rules.
Not the roles.
Not the reputation.
Relationship is the destination.
Everything else is just a sign pointing toward it.
And I don't want to live at the billboard anymore.
I want the real thing.

## Questions to honestly ponder

Where in my life am I obeying a system, role, or
expectation about God instead of responding to the living
presence of Christ—and what am I afraid would unravel if I
let Him lead me there instead?
If you want something even more surgical—something that
strips the last hiding places—here's a second layer you can
sit with slowly:

What part of my faith life would feel unsafe, exposed, or
unnecessary if I stopped managing my spirituality and
trusted Jesus Himself to rule my heart—and am I willing to
let that thing die so real relationship can live?

These are not questions to answer quickly.
They are questions to sit with...
to let ache...
to let dismantle.
Because whatever truth they uncover is not there to shame
us—
it's there to set us free.

## Prayer

Father,
I'm not coming to You with polished words today.
I'm coming tired.
I'm coming a little disappointed—
not in You, but in how often I've settled for knowing about
You instead of knowing You.
I've learned the language.
I've memorized the truths.
I've respected the systems that taught me how to recognize
You, name You, and honor You.
And I'm grateful for them. Truly.
They carried me here.
But they were never meant to replace You.
Somewhere along the way, I noticed my hands were full of
answers
and my heart was still hungry.
I knew the right things to say,
but I wasn't always crawling into Your presence and just
being with You.
And that ache—that quiet ache—has been telling the
truth.So here I am. No formula. No checklist. No
bargaining.
I just want You.
I want the kind of relationship that doesn't need to prove
itself.
The kind that breathes.
The kind that rests.
The kind where I don't have to manage You or perform for
You or figure You out before I'm allowed close.
I want to sit in Your lap and let You be God without asking
You to earn that place in my life—
because You already have.

Forgive me for the ways I've leaned on structure when You
were inviting surrender.
Forgive me for mistaking discipline for intimacy, and
effort for love.
Thank You for the teachers, the churches, the words, the
paths that pointed me toward You—
and thank You that none of them are You.
You never asked me to build a life around religion.
You asked me to walk with You.
And God—there's joy here.
Real joy.
Not the loud, forced kind, but the deep, steady kind that
bubbles up when I realize I'm already held.
That I'm already known.
That I don't have to climb to be close.
Let this freedom be contagious.
Let others see the ease, the honesty, the warmth of a life
rooted in relationship—not obligation.
Let them know there is room in Your presence for their
questions, their weariness, their longing.
If anyone comes after me, let them find a God who
welcomes, not demands.
A Father who opens His arms, not His ledger.
A love that invites us closer, not busier.
I choose You again—not as a concept, not as a system, not
as a transaction—
but as my Father.
I'm here.
I'm listening.
And I'm not getting out of Your lap anytime soon.
Amen

# Invitation Eight: To Release the Cords

"Forgive us our debts, as we forgive our debtors."
(Matthew 6:12)
This is one of the hardest prayers Jesus ever taught us to
pray.
Not because it's confusing. But because it's honest.
It's easy to say, "I forgive." It's much harder to notice when
we're still replaying the offense, turning it over in our
minds, revisiting the pain, rehearsing the injustice.
And when I'm still doing that—when the offense still has a
grip on my thoughts—I know something hasn't been
released yet. There is still an entanglement.
Part of what makes forgiveness so difficult is that we often
know the other person deserves consequences. Their words
mattered. Their actions caused harm. What was done
cannot be undone.
Some of us were taught that forgiveness means pretending
none of that mattered. Others were taught that forgiveness
means restoring closeness or trust.
But Jesus never said either of those things.
Forgiving someone does not mean justifying what they did.
Forgiving someone does not mean forgetting what
happened. Forgiving someone does not mean placing
yourself back into harm's way.
Forgiveness is not reconciliation. Forgiveness is release.
When Jesus taught this prayer in Aramaic, the language
carries a depth that's easy to miss in English. The idea is
this:
Unburden me from my heavy obligations and failures
toward You, just as I release the binding cords of another's
guilt toward me.

That word picture matters.

Unforgiveness is like holding cords—binding cords—that keep another person tied to us. But those same cords are wrapped around us as well. As long as I'm gripping them, I am entangled. And here's the hard truth: If I refuse to untangle those cords—to release another from their guilt toward me—I cannot expect God to fully untangle me from my own guilt and sin.

That's why this prayer is so sobering.

I've walked through a kind of harm that wasn't accidental. It wasn't careless. It was deliberate. Planned. Intended to wound deeply—mentally, emotionally, physically, financially. My family and I were altered by it in ways that can't simply be erased.

And for a long time, holding unforgiveness felt justified. There's a saying that unforgiveness is like drinking poison and waiting for the other person to die. That's not far off—but the deeper truth is this: unforgiveness keeps me bound to the very person who harmed me.

I don't want that.

Recently, God showed me something that changed how I see this entirely.

My family belongs to Him. We are His children.

So when someone plotted against us—when they worked intentionally to harm us—they weren't only offending us. They were offending the heart of God. They were harming His kids.

And suddenly, I realized: this is not mine to carry anymore.

When someone harms my children, my instinct is fierce protection and justice on their behalf. And God's heart toward His children is infinitely more protective, more righteous, more capable than mine could ever be.

So forgiveness, for me, looks like this:

"God, I untangle this person from their offense against me and my family. I release them from my judgment. Whatever consequences come from their actions are Yours to handle, not mine. I do not wish them harm. I do not seek an outcome. I am letting go."

That doesn't erase the damage. It doesn't minimize the pain. It doesn't mean everything is suddenly healed.

But it does mean I am no longer bound.

Forgiveness, I'm learning, often happens in layers.

I forgive as deeply as I'm able today. Then I sit in God's lap. I let Him show me His view—of me, of my family, of the other person, of the harm itself.

And days later, sometimes, I find I can forgive more deeply. Not because I forced it, but because God untangled something else inside me.

What I know for certain is this: I cannot free myself while still gripping the cords.

When I truly forgive, the cords fall away. The entanglement breaks. The curse of sin loses its grip on my life and my family.

And whether or not the other person ever repents, apologizes, or changes—I walk free.

That freedom is not cheap. But it is real. And it is worth everything.

## Question to prayerfully consider

Who am I still bound to because I am holding them
accountable in ways only God was meant to carry—and am
I willing to release them, without justifying their actions, so
that both they and I can be fully placed back into God's
hands and finally walk free?

Is there someone whose offense I am still gripping—
knowing their actions were wrong and harmful—and am I
willing to untangle myself from them, not to excuse what
they did, but to free God's hands to do His work in both
their life and mine, releasing me from the entanglement
that keeps us bound together?

## Prayer

God, I come to You without pretending this is easy.
You see the cords I've been holding— the ones wrapped
around pain, injustice, and harm that should never have
happened. You know how tightly they've been wound, how
long I've carried them, how much strength it's taken just to
survive what was done.
I'm not excusing what happened. I'm not calling wrong
things right. I'm not pretending the damage didn't matter.
But today, I am choosing release.
With trembling hands, I place this person into Your care. I
untangle myself from their guilt toward me. I lay down the
burden of judgment, vengeance, and outcome. What they
did against me—and against Your heart—belongs to You
now.
This is Your work. Not mine.
I acknowledge how hard this is, God. How layered
forgiveness feels. How fear tries to convince me that letting
go will leave me exposed.
But You are my provider. You are my protector. You are
my healer.

Nothing I release into Your hands is lost. Nothing I entrust to You is neglected. Nothing You hold remains unfinished. So I thank You—deeply, reverently—for the freedom You are giving me. Freedom in my thoughts. Freedom in my body. Freedom in my spirit. Freedom from being bound to what harmed me.

I choose to walk forward unentangled. Unburdened. Unbound.

Whatever comes from this point on— whether justice, repentance, consequence, or silence— I am free from it, because I am Yours.

Bring healing where there has been wounding. Bring reassurance where there has been fear. Bring protection where there has been exposure. Bring restitution in ways only You can accomplish.

I trust You with my life. I trust You with my future. I trust You with eternity.

And today, by Your grace, I walk free— now and forever.
Amen

# Invitation Nine: To Steward What is Holy

Ephesians 5:15–16 (Amplified)
"Therefore see that you walk carefully [living life with honor, purpose, and courage...], not as the unwise, but as wise... making the very most of your time [on earth], because the days are [filled with] evil."
I don't want to manage my time.
I want to steward it.
Management feels tight and anxious—like if I don't control every minute, something will fall apart. Stewardship feels different. Stewardship acknowledges that my time is a gift God has entrusted to me, meant to be handled with wisdom, joy, and intention.
So today, I'm crawling up into God's lap again and asking a very honest question:
"How do You want me to spend the time You've given me?"
Not how do I squeeze more in. Not how do I become endlessly productive. But how do I live wisely.
Ephesians urges us to walk carefully—not fearfully, not rigidly, but intentionally. To live with discernment. To recognize that our days are limited, meaningful, and often filled with quiet opportunities that don't announce themselves loudly.
And this is where I need to be honest with myself.
How much of my time is being swallowed by distraction? How often do I stay busy to feel safe or necessary? How much margin do I actually leave for people—for interruptions, for moments that cannot be scheduled?
I want structure—but not so much that I become unavailable.
Because some people I encounter, I may only meet once. Some walk through my life for a very short season. And I don't want to miss those moments because I was so locked into my agenda that I couldn't be fully present.

Sometimes what people need most isn't answers or solutions. They need someone to see them. To listen. To lift them to God quietly in intercession.

That kind of presence requires margin.

At the same time, I don't believe God calls us to drift through life without preparation or intention. Scripture is clear about the value of diligence:

Proverbs 21:5

"The plans of the diligent lead surely to abundance, but everyone who is hasty comes only to poverty."

That verse doesn't celebrate busyness. It honors thoughtful, steady faithfulness.

Biblical planning isn't about squeezing every ounce of productivity out of a day. It's about creating a structure that helps me know where I'm going—so I don't live rushed, reactive, or scattered along the way.

Planning gives me a framework. God fills in the journey. I can know the destination—and still allow God to shape how I travel between here and there.

That flexibility matters more than I sometimes realize.

Today, I lost a friend.

We didn't have long conversations or a lot of shared time. But I am profoundly grateful for how one moment was used.

During a candlelight service, a week ago, I spoke from my heart—sharing about light, life, and the sacrifice of Christ. I didn't know how it would be received. I simply trusted God with what He had placed in me to say.

My friend was attentive. Quiet. Present.

A few days later, he reached out to thank me. He told me that what was shared had been deeply impactful—that it felt like a rebirth experience for him.

I sat with that for a long moment.

Had I been too busy, too distracted, or too focused on keeping things light and surface-level, that moment might have passed untouched. But because there was space—because there was margin—God was able to use it to draw a heart toward Himself.

I am deeply grateful for that.
And it has caused me to pause and consider just how brief our time here really is—and how quietly urgent it can be.
Not an urgency driven by pressure, but one shaped by love.
An urgency that whispers: don't be so busy that you miss the moment God is already working in.
That's what stewarding time wisely looks like to me.
It's planning with diligence. Walking with flexibility.
Leaving room for God to interrupt my agenda with eternal purpose.
That's why Matthew 6:33 keeps pulling me back:
"Seek first the kingdom of God and His righteousness, and all these things will be added to you."
When I seek God first—not out of duty, not to earn favor—everything else has the chance to stay in its proper place.
I don't want to start my day with Him just to say I did my part. I want to start my day hungry for Him.
I want that time with God to be so natural and life-giving that my day feels incomplete without it—not because of guilt, but because of desire.
When I seek Him first in that way, my time doesn't feel scattered. It feels aligned.
So today isn't about fixing a schedule.
It's about surrendering it.
It's about asking God to help me steward my time in a way that honors Him, blesses others, and still allows me to live fully and joyfully in the life He's given me.
Because time is holy ground.
And I want to walk on it wisely.

## Question to ponder

When I look honestly at how I spend my time, what does it reveal about what I'm truly seeking—and where might God be inviting me to create margin so I don't miss the people and moments He has entrusted to me?
If you'd like a slightly more searching alternative:
Where have I filled my days so tightly that there's no room left for God's interruptions—and what might change if I trusted Him enough to leave space for what matters eternally?

## Prayer

God, I bring You my time— not just the hours I feel generous enough to give, but the ones I guard, defend, and justify.
I bring You my agenda. The plans I cling to because they make me feel safe. The structure I hide behind when I'm afraid of slowing down. The busyness I use to avoid listening too closely.
I confess that sometimes I would rather stay productive than stay present. I would rather stay in motion than risk being interrupted by You.
But You see what lives underneath that.
You see the fear of wasting time. The fear of missing something important. The fear that if I loosen my grip, everything will fall apart.
So today, I loosen my hands.I release the need to control outcomes. I release the pressure to make every moment prove my worth. I release the illusion that urgency equals obedience.

Teach me how to steward my time the way You do— with wisdom, not haste; with intention, not rigidity; with diligence, not striving.
Show me where I have crowded You out with schedules that leave no room for relationship. Show me where I have mistaken activity for faithfulness.
And then, gently, reorder me.
Help me seek You first— not out of duty, not as a transaction, but out of hunger.
Let my days begin with You and bend toward You as they unfold. Let my plans be held loosely enough for You to reshape them with eternal purpose.
Give me eyes to see the moments that matter. Give me courage to pause when love is required. Give me grace to trust that nothing surrendered to You is ever lost.
I place my time back into Your hands. I place my agenda back under Your care. I choose presence over pressure, trust over control, relationship over routine.
Lead me, God. I will follow— even when it means slowing down, even when it means changing course, even when it reaches places I've avoided.
My time is Yours. My life is Yours. And I trust You with both.
Amen

# Day Ten: To Linger

Matthew 13:13–14 (Amplified)
"This is the reason I speak to the crowds in parables: because while [having the power of] seeing they do not see, and while [having the power of] hearing they do not hear, nor do they understand and grasp [spiritual things]. You will hear and keep on hearing, but never understand; And you will look and keep on looking, but never comprehend."
There's something in this passage that stops me every time.
Jesus isn't saying the people can't see or hear. He's saying they do—and still miss it.
They're present physically, but not inwardly.
And I don't ever want that to be true of me.
I don't want to see and see and see, yet never truly comprehend. I don't want to hear and hear and hear, but somehow miss what God is actually saying.
When the disciples asked Jesus why He spoke in parables, this was His answer. And it tells me something important: understanding isn't just about exposure—it's about remaining. About being present long enough for what we're seeing and hearing to actually sink in.
I want to be one of the ones who stays.
When I'm with God, I don't want my body in the moment while my mind is elsewhere—replaying the past, reprocessing old conclusions, or running ahead into the what-ifs of the future. Even good reflections can become distractions if they pull me away from what He's offering now.
I want to be steeped in this moment.
And the image that keeps coming to mind is something simple—pickles.
Cucumbers don't become pickles by being dipped into brine and pulled back out. They aren't transformed by a quick encounter. They're transformed by soaking. By remaining. By staying in the brine long enough that something fundamental changes.

If you drop a cucumber into brine for a moment and remove it, it still tastes like a cucumber.
But if it stays— if it remains— it slowly takes on the flavor of the brine itself.
That's what I want for my life with God.
Not quick moments of inspiration. Not passing encounters. But lingering presence.
I don't want to rush through time with Him and call it connection. I want to remain there—quiet, attentive, receptive—until something in me actually changes.
And I want the same kind of presence with people.
I get a limited amount of time with the people God places in my life. We're given some measure of life together—and then that season ends. I don't want to skim those moments. I want to soak in them.
I want to remain present long enough to truly experience who they are—how they think, how they see the world, how they respond, what delights them, what weighs on them. I want to receive the gift of their presence with gratitude.
Not in a consuming way. In a reverent way.
I get to experience this person.
That's not a small thing.
Presence—real presence—changes the quality of everything.
Laughter deepens. Conversation slows. Silence becomes comfortable instead of awkward.
Whether the moment is playful and light or quiet and vulnerable, I don't want to dip in and rush out. I want to remain until the moment has done its work.
Because transformation doesn't happen by passing through.
It happens by staying.
This is what I hear Jesus saying beneath these words: Don't just hear—remain until you understand. Don't just look— stay until you comprehend.

I don't want to live my life tasting like a cucumber when I've been invited to become something entirely different.
So today, I'm choosing to remain. To stay present. To soak. With God. With people. With this moment right here. Because this is where transformation happens— not by rushing through, but by lingering long enough for love, truth, and connection to fully take hold.
This is how I want to live— seeing and comprehending, hearing and understanding, fully present.

**Question to Ponder**

Where in my life am I dipping in and rushing out—of moments with God or people—and what might change if I chose to remain present long enough for real transformation to occur?
What would it look like for me to stay fully present in the moments I'm usually tempted to rush through, and how might that deepen my connection with God and the people He's placed in my life?

**Prayer**

God, I confess how quickly I rush.
I rush through moments with You. I rush through moments with people. I rush through stillness because it feels inefficient, and through silence because it asks something of me.
I don't always want to remain. Sometimes I want the effect without the soaking. The transformation without the waiting. The fruit without the surrender.
But You know that about me already.
So I'm not pretending here.
I bring You my impatience. I bring You my distractions. I bring You the part of me that wants to dip in, gather just enough, and move on unchanged.
And I ask You—gently, persistently— to woo me into staying.
Teach me how to remain with You long enough that Your life actually seeps into mine. Long enough that my thoughts begin to taste like Yours. That my responses carry Your fragrance. That my presence reflects Your character.
I don't want to just look like someone who has been near You. I want to be changed by You.
Help me remain when it's uncomfortable. Help me stay when nothing dramatic is happening. Help me trust that transformation is taking place even when I can't feel it yet.
And as You do this work in me, let it be evident—not in performance, but in presence.
Let others encounter something in me that makes them curious. That makes them linger. That makes them desire to remain in You as well.
Not because I have done this well, but because You have been faithful.
I choose to stay. I choose to soak. I choose to trust that You are at work beneath the surface.
Make my life taste like You. So that the world, encountering Your goodness through me, wants to remain too.
Amen

# Invitation Eleven: To Trust God for This Moment

When I picture myself crawling up into God's lap, the first thing I become aware of is how loud my mind is.
It chatters.
It rehearses.
It replays old stories.
It whispers fears and half-truths.
It clings to conclusions I made long ago, often for survival.
And I've learned something about myself: as long as my mind is that loud, my heart can't really hear.
So I sit.
I stay.
Not forcing silence—but allowing it. Letting God hold the space long enough for the noise to settle.
And when it finally does, when the chatter softens just enough, something shifts in me.
My posture changes.
I picture myself lifting my hands toward Him—open, empty, honest—and offering Him everything I have. Not symbolically. Sincerely.
I want to give Him all my love.
All my joy.
All my peace.
All my patience.
All my kindness.
All my goodness.
All my gentleness.
All my faithfulness.
All my self-control.
All my time.
All my life.
And if I stay there long enough, a realization quietly settles in.

The only love I have to offer Him is the love He first gave me.
The only joy I lift back to Him is joy He placed in me.
The only peace I know is peace He breathed into my chaos.
The patience I've learned—He developed.
The kindness I extend—He showed me first.
Even my time isn't mine.
Every moment I give Him is a moment He is already sustaining. Without His voice holding my life together, I don't even have another breath, let alone another moment to surrender.
Psalm 24 reminds me of this truth plainly:
"The earth is the Lord's, and everything in it."
Everything.
Including me.
Including every moment I've been given.
Creation itself came into being by the sound of His voice, and it is that same voice that continues to sustain it.
Nothing I possess—no strength, no insight, no resource, no fruit of my life—originated with me.
Paul echoes it again in 1 Corinthians:
"The earth is the Lord's, and everything in it."
And suddenly, surrender doesn't feel like loss.
It feels like alignment.
Nothing I'm offering Him was ever truly mine. I'm not handing Him something I produced—I'm returning what He entrusted to me.
That changes everything.
Because if He is the source, I don't need to hoard.
If He is the source, generosity doesn't deplete me.
If He is the source, giving doesn't diminish—it multiplies.
When I extend grace, I'm not running out.
When I give my time, I'm not losing it.
When I share light, it doesn't dim.
I'm stewarding what belongs to Him.
And this applies to more than time, money, or talents.

Even the fruits of the Spirit—the love, joy, peace, patience, kindness, goodness, faithfulness, gentleness, self-control that bubble up within me—are gifts that emerge naturally when I remain connected to Him.
I think of a fruit tree.
The tree doesn't strain.
It doesn't perform.
It doesn't anxiously try to produce.
It simply remains rooted in life.
The fruit appears because the connection is intact.
Those fruits can fall to the ground and rot.
Or they can be plucked and enjoyed—nourishing the world around them.
But the tree never produces the fruit by effort.
And neither do I.
As someone who has surrendered my life to Christ, who has accepted His sacrifice and chosen to remain connected to Him, the fruit of His life will grow in me—unless I sever that connection.
My role isn't production.
It's remaining.
And when I remain, His life flows through me for the sake of others.
That's why the prayer that keeps returning to me is simple and steady:
Give us today what we need for today.
Not tomorrow's provision.
Not next year's clarity.
Not answers for every unknown.
Just what is needed for this moment.
Because Philippians 4:19 reminds me:
"My God will supply every need according to His riches in glory."
Not scraped together.
Not rationed.
Not measured cautiously.

According to His riches—riches without limit, without
shortage, without fear of running out.
This moment has been given.
This breath has been sustained.
This life is being held.
And living generously inside this moment—trusting Him
for the moment itself—may be one of the most faithful
offerings I can make.
I don't have to clutch what was never mine.
I don't have to fear giving what He continues to supply.
I only need to remain.

**Question to Ponder**

What would change in the way I give—my time, my
presence, my patience, my love, my resources—if I truly
believed that nothing I offer is being depleted, but
multiplied, because God is the source and I am simply
stewarding what already belongs to Him?

If you'd like an even more inward, quietly unsettling
option:
Where am I still holding tightly to something God has
entrusted to me—and what might generosity look like
there if I trusted that giving would multiply, not diminish,
what He supplies?

**Prayer**

God, I come to You empty-handed.
Not pretending I've figured this out.
Not pretending I've been generous without fear.
Not pretending I've trusted You as fully as I want to.
I see how tightly I hold things You never asked me to own.
Time.
Energy.
Provision.
Even the good fruit You've grown in me.

Sometimes I act like if I let go, I'll run out.
Like if I give too much, there won't be enough left.
Like somehow the supply depends on me.
And that's not true—but it feels true in my body
sometimes.
So I bring You that fear.
The fear of depletion.
The fear of scarcity.
The fear that generosity will cost me more than I can
afford.
I lay it down here.
Because everything I have comes from You.
Every breath.
Every moment.
Every ounce of love, patience, peace, strength, clarity.
Every opportunity to give.
None of it is mine to hoard.
All of it is Yours to steward.
Teach me to live open-handed.
Not reckless. Not careless.
But confident—because You are the source.
When I give, remind me I am not losing.
When I share, remind me You are multiplying.
When I feel empty, remind me You are still supplying.
Help me remain connected to You—not striving to
produce,
but trusting that Your life in me will naturally bear fruit
meant to nourish the world around me.
I don't want to clutch what was never mine.
I don't want to fear giving what You freely provide.
I want to live as someone who believes You—
fully, deeply, and without reserve.
So take what I'm offering now—
even my uncertainty, even my fear—
and teach me how to steward Your gifts with joy.
I choose to remain.
I choose to trust.
I choose to live from abundance, not lack.
Amen

# Invitation Twelve: A Holy Pause

Before we move forward, let's stop here for a moment.
Not to rush into the next idea.
Not to tie everything up neatly.
But to linger—just a little longer—in what God has already
been stirring within us.
As we come to the end of these first days together, I want to
pause—not to conclude, but to remember.
To remember where we began.
We didn't start with resolve or ambition.
We didn't start with goals, plans, or promises to do better.
We started with humility.
We started by admitting imbalance.
By acknowledging buried places.
By letting God search us instead of fixing ourselves.
We chose relationship over religion—leaving the billboard
and turning our hearts toward the real destination:
nearness. We remembered that knowing about God is not
the same as knowing Him, and that intimacy cannot be
replaced by systems, formulas, or good standing.
We began loosening our grip.
We learned to release the cords—to forgive not by
minimizing harm, but by untangling ourselves from it. To
trust God with justice, protection, and outcomes, so that we
could walk free even while wounds were still tender.
We remembered that our time is holy ground—not
something to control anxiously, but something to steward
wisely. We leaned toward diligence and margin, leaving
space for God to interrupt our agendas with eternal
purpose.
We practiced lingering—to remain present long enough for
transformation to actually occur. To soak rather than skim.
To stay with God, with people, and with moments until
something real changed within us.

And finally, we were drawn into trusting God for this moment—surrendering not only outcomes, but the breath, the strength, the fruit, and the resources we so easily clutch out of fear. We remembered that everything we offer back to Him was first given by Him, and that remaining connected is where life flows.
Taken together, these invitations were never asking us to do more.
They were asking us to live differently.
To shift the paradigm from which we function.
To notice what motivates us.
To become aware of where we are striving instead of remaining.
To recognize where fear, urgency, or habit may be shaping our days more than trust and love.
And something important has happened along the way.
These days were never meant to be a checklist.
They were never meant to become a system.
They were never meant to turn into resolutions we strain to keep.
This isn't about trying harder.
It's about remaining.
What God has been doing in these moments is not superficial work. It's not behavior modification. It's not polishing the outside. It's the quiet, faithful work of transformation—work that happens when we stay connected to Him long enough for His life to become our life.
And that kind of transformation doesn't come from effort. It comes from relationship.
The truths we've lingered in—about balance, surrender, forgiveness, generosity, presence—these aren't things you now have to maintain by force. They are truths God is settling into you as you stay close to Him.

They become part of who you are.
Not because you resolved to change.
But because you remained connected to the Source of life.
There will be days when imbalance tries to creep back in.
Days when old fears whisper again.
Days when distractions feel louder than truth.
That doesn't mean you've failed.
It simply means you return.
Back to humility.
Back to curiosity instead of judgment.
Back to the lap you already know is waiting.
This is how lasting change happens—
not in dramatic leaps, but in faithful returning.
Not by striving upward, but by staying rooted.
So let this pause be a place of rest.
A place of listening.
A place where seeds can settle deeper.
Take a breath.
There is no rush here.
No expectation to fix, solve, or improve anything.
These questions are not invitations to strive deeper—but to
notice, to allow, and to surrender. You may sit with one.
You may circle back to another later. Let God choose
which ones press gently on your heart today.

## Questions to Sit With

- Where in my life has religion quietly replaced relationship—and what would it look like to crawl back into God's lap in that place?
- Are there cords I am still holding—judgments, replayed offenses, or self-protection—that God is inviting me to release so I can walk more freely?

- How am I currently stewarding my time: from anxiety and control, or from trust and alignment with God's purposes?
- Where do I tend to rush—through prayer, through people, through moments—when God may be inviting me to linger instead?
- What would change in my daily life if remaining connected to God became my primary responsibility, rather than producing outcomes or proving faithfulness?
- In this present moment, what is God already supplying that I can trust Him for—without reaching ahead for tomorrow's provision?
- 

**Beneath the Surface**

(Lingering a Little Longer)
Remain here as long as you need.
You don't need to force clarity.
You don't need to rush resolution.
Sometimes growth feels measurable.
Sometimes it feels subtle.
Sometimes it feels like peace instead of progress.
All of it counts.
Remain curious.
Remain honest.
Remain open.
And sit with these, slowly:

- What parts of myself do I most instinctively try to manage, control, or protect—and what might God be inviting me to surrender there instead?
- Where have I been defining myself by strengths or gifts that God may be asking to transform rather than remove?
- What am I afraid God might see if I stop filtering myself—and what does that fear reveal about how I currently view Him?

- What patterns, reactions, or habits have I labeled as "just the way I am," that God may be gently inviting me to see differently?
- If I allowed myself to be seen by God exactly as I am today—no polishing, no hiding—what part of me feels most exposed, and what does that part need from Him?
- What would change if I trusted that God is not threatened by my broken places, nor impressed by my strengths—but deeply committed to transforming both?
- Where do I sense potential in myself that feels confusing, heavy, or even burdensome—and how might God want to reframe that potential through His eyes instead of mine?
- What is one area of my life where I feel stuck—and am I willing to let God show me whether that place needs pruning, healing, or simply patience?
- If nothing in me were wasted, what might God be growing beneath the surface that I can't fully see yet?

There is no "right" outcome here.
You are not performing for God.
You are being formed by Him.
You are not managing your transformation.
You are participating in it.
You are not carrying this alone.
You never were.
As long as you remain connected to Him—
as long as you keep soaking in who He is—
these truths will continue to shape you quietly, steadily, eternally.
And over time, without effort or announcement, your life will begin to reflect Him in ways that feel natural and true.

Not because you tried.
But because you stayed.
So keep coming back.
Keep crawling up.
Keep remaining.
This isn't the end of the work.
It's the rhythm of a life lived connected to the Source of all
light, life, and love.
And that—more than anything else—
is where transformation continues.

**Prayer**

God, I come to You gently today.
Not braced.
Not performing.
Not afraid of what You might see.
I come as I am—
because I already belong.
Thank You for being a God who invites me closer instead
of pushing me away.
Thank You for the safety of Your presence, for the way You
welcome me into Your lap—not to correct me harshly, but
to hold me securely while You do Your beautiful work.
Help me be generous with myself, the way You are
generous with me.
Help me stop shaming what You are patiently
transforming.
Help me trust that when You invite me to look more
closely, it is never for exposure's sake—it is always for
healing.
Thank You for who You are in me.
For Your Spirit living within me.
For Christ in me—the hope of glory.
Thank You that my identity is not fragile.

It is anchored.
It is settled.
It is secure in You.
Jesus, thank You for paying the price I could never pay.
Thank You for stepping into my place, for giving
everything so that I could be welcomed fully, freely, and
forever into the heart of the Father.
Thank You for opening the way—not just to forgiveness,
but to relationship.
Father, thank You for Your generosity.
For the daily provision I sometimes overlook.

For the moment-by-moment sustaining of my life.
For giving me what I need—even when I don't yet know
how to ask for it.
Thank You for giving so lavishly that it looked like heaven
was emptied for my sake—
and yet knowing that Your resources never diminish,
never weaken, never run dry.
Thank You that even the act of crawling up into Your lap
carries eternal purpose.
That rest is not wasted.
That reflection is not indulgent.
That surrender is not passive.
Everything You do in me is for transformation.
And that transformation is good.
It pleases Your heart—and in time, it brings joy, freedom,
and life to mine, and to everyone my life touches.
So I rest here.
Grateful.
Open.
Trusting.
Continue Your work in me, at Your pace, in Your way.
I am safe in Your hands.
Amen

# Invitation Thirteen: Honoring the Body as Sacred Space

Lately, God has been gently reminding me of something I've known for a long time—but haven't always held with the attention it deserves.

My body is not separate from my spiritual life. It is not secondary. It is not an inconvenience to manage while I focus on "more important" things.

It is the place where the Holy Spirit lives.

Paul says it plainly in 1 Corinthians 6:19–20: my body is a temple of the Holy Spirit. I am not my own. I was bought with a price. That truth isn't meant to create pressure or fear—it's meant to invite reverence, care, and gratitude.

This body matters to God.

And honoring Him through the way I live in this body—through nourishment, rest, movement, discipline, enjoyment, and wisdom—is not vanity.

It is worship.

Romans 12:1 calls this a living sacrifice. Not a reluctant one. Not a worn-down one. Not a joyless one governed by rigid rules. A willing, living offering.

That tells me something important: God isn't asking me to punish my body or obsess over it. He's inviting me to enjoy it—to steward it—to live in alignment with how He designed it to function.

I'm realizing that caring well for my body is an expression of gratitude.

Not a checklist. Not a burden. Not a set of rules to follow under pressure.

But a daily "thank You."

Thank You for life. Thank You for breath. Thank You for strength. Thank You for the ability to move, to heal, to recover, to enjoy.

I don't want to merely exist inside this body—I want to fully enjoy it. I want to live every day of the life God has given me as healthy as possible, not because I fear illness, but because I value the gift.

I want to run and play with my great-grandchildren someday. I don't want to sit on the sidelines wishing I could participate. I want to be active, engaged, present, and capable—able to serve God and love people with energy and joy.

That means giving this body what it needs.

Movement that feels like play. Food that nourishes instead of depletes. Rest that repairs instead of being postponed. Sleep that restores. Healthy processing of stress instead of storing it.

Because stress—unprocessed, unspoken, unresolved—doesn't stay abstract. I carry it in tissue, in tension, in fatigue. My body remembers what my mind tries to ignore.

Jeremiah 30:17 reminds me of God's heart here: "I will restore you to health and heal your wounds," declares the Lord.

Healing matters to Him. Balance matters to Him. Wholeness matters to Him.

At the same time, Matthew 6:25 keeps me from tipping into control or fear: Do not worry about your life... what you will eat or drink... or about your body.

So again, there's that holy balance.

Care deeply—but don't obsess. Be disciplined—but don't strive. Be mindful—but don't be afraid
I think of it like an engine built by someone who knows exactly how it works. If the creator gives clear guidance on fuel, maintenance, and care, following those guidelines isn't restrictive—it's wise. Ignoring them doesn't create freedom; it just leads to breakdown.
God created this body. He knows how it thrives. Movement isn't punishment—it's joy. Eating well isn't deprivation—it's nourishment. Rest isn't laziness—it's repair.
Jumping on a trampoline with grandchildren. Kicking a ball. Climbing trees. Laughing hard. Sleeping deeply. This is how this body was meant to live.
I've noticed that lately, busyness has nudged me a bit out of balance—not because I stopped caring, but because convenience crept in. Skipped rest. Rushed choices. Less intention than I want.
So I'm bringing this too back into the Father's lap. Not with shame. Not with frustration. But with trust.
I'm asking Him for wisdom—how to care for this body with joy. How to design my life so that health feels natural and life-giving, not like another task to manage.
I believe that building a strong immune system, honoring how this body heals, and caring for it well is part of partnering with God—not replacing Him. I trust Him with my health, while also doing what He has shown me helps this body flourish.
This kind of care allows me to serve Him better. It allows me to love people better. It allows me to steward the time He's given me here with gratitude.
This isn't about perfection. It's about alignment. And I trust that the One who created my body is faithful to show me how to care for it with joy, freedom, and balance.

## Question

If I viewed caring for my body as an act of grateful worship rather than obligation, what one area—rest, nourishment, movement, stress, or rhythm—might God be inviting me to bring back into joyful alignment with how He designed me to live?
What is my body quietly asking for right now—and how might responding with gratitude instead of discipline change the way I care for it?

## Prayer

Father, thank You for this body You have given me. Thank You for breath that fills my lungs, for a heart that keeps beating, for muscles that move, for nerves that feel, for senses that allow me to experience this world You created.
Thank You that this body is not an afterthought to You. It is a sacred place where Your Spirit lives. It is worthy of care, attention, and honor—not because it must be perfect, but because it is Yours.
I release shame today. Shame for what I haven't done well. Shame for seasons of imbalance. Shame for choices made out of hurry or exhaustion.
You are not disappointed in me. You are inviting me into healing.
Teach me how to trust You with my health— to care deeply without fear, to be disciplined without striving, to be mindful without obsession.
Help me listen to my body with kindness. Help me respond with gratitude instead of criticism. Help me enjoy caring for this body as an act of worship— a quiet "thank You" lived out in daily choices.

I trust You as my healer. I trust You as my provider. I trust You as the One who restores balance when things are out of alignment.
When I need rest, lead me into it. When I need movement, let it feel like joy. When I need nourishment, guide me with wisdom and freedom. When stress presses in, help me release it into Your hands instead of storing it within myself.
Thank You that You desire wholeness for me— body, soul, and spirit. Thank You that healing is part of Your heart. Thank You that caring for myself allows me to serve You and love others more fully.
I offer this body back to You today—not as a burden, but as a living, grateful sacrifice. Use it as You will. Sustain it as only You can.
I rest in Your care. I trust Your wisdom. I receive Your healing.
Amen

# Invitation Fourteen: Learning to Live with Grief

Grief is one of the strangest companions I've ever known. When my husband passed away—just short of three years ago now—grief felt wild and intrusive. The best way I know how to describe it is this: it was like bringing a high-energy puppy into my home.

Before the front door even opens, everyone is already bracing themselves. The puppy is thrilled—so thrilled that its joy is almost dangerous. It's jumping, scratching, nipping, knocking things out of hands. Kids end up crying. Someone gets knocked to the floor. Normal life becomes nearly impossible—not because the puppy is bad, but because it doesn't yet know how to exist within the rhythms of the home.

That's what grief was like at first.

It was in my face constantly. It knocked me flat.

It interrupted everything.

It made simple tasks feel overwhelming.

Not because grief was wrong—but because it was raw, untrained, and enormous.

And in that place, I learned something precious: God was not distant.

Scripture says the Lord is close to the brokenhearted. Not standing across the room. Not waiting for composure. Close. When my heart felt shattered beyond repair, He did not recoil. He leaned in.

You don't train grief the way you train a dog. You don't command it. You don't silence it. You don't control it.

But you do learn how to live with it.

Over time, as a puppy grows, something shifts. The puppy learns the rhythms of the household. It learns what is safe, what is welcome, what is gentle. It no longer has to clamber for every ounce of attention or reassurance. It settles—not because it is less alive, but because it is secure.

Grief followed a similar path for me.
That first year, it was invasive and relentless.
The second year, it became something I learned how to carry within daily life.
There were still moments—sudden ones—where it would leap forward unexpectedly. But those moments were shorter. Less destructive. More contained.
By a year and a half, two years in, grief became something I could live with—not just tolerate, but understand.
And eventually, something even more surprising happened.
Grief stopped being only about missing him.
It became about treasuring him.
Not just who he was when he was here—but how the beauty he brought into my life continues to shape every part of it. His joy. His curiosity. His industriousness. His excitement for building, learning, creating. His legacy.
Scripture says God heals the brokenhearted and binds up their wounds. I've learned that this binding is not rushed. It is tender. It is deliberate. It is patient. God does not demand that grief disappear—He tends it until it no longer bleeds uncontrollably.
When you love someone deeply, you are entrusted with their life.
And when they are gone, you are entrusted with their grief. That is a holy trust.
Grief is not something to be crushed under.
It is not something to avoid.
It is not something to let flatten you indefinitely.
It is something to carry with purpose.
And God does not ask us to carry it alone.
Again and again, He reminds us not to be afraid, not because pain isn't real, but because He is present. He strengthens us. He upholds us. When grief weakens our knees and steals our breath, He supplies what we cannot.
Believers still grieve—but we grieve with hope.

Death does not get the final word.
The resurrection of Jesus assures us that death is not the end of the story. God promises a future where He Himself will wipe away every tear—where there will be no more death, no more mourning, no more crying, no more pain. That promise does not erase today's sorrow, but it anchors it. It keeps grief from turning into hopelessness.
Because there is always—always—purpose in the pain.
We can let loss knock us down and leave us spiraling in despair.
Or we can allow God to meet us in the sorrow and do something redemptive with it.
One of the most unexpected gifts grief has given me is this: it has expanded my capacity for compassion. Scripture says that God comforts us in our troubles so that we can comfort others with the same comfort we have received.
What we survive does not have to end with us. It can become a place of ministry—quiet, gentle, and deeply authentic.
Grief never disappears.
But when it is held with care, it matures.
Just like that puppy who once knocked everyone over eventually learns to walk in step with the household, grief—when processed healthfully—learns how to live alongside life instead of overtaking it.
It never diminishes love.
It honors it.
This invitation is not about getting over grief.
It is about learning how to live faithfully with it.
How to let it settle into its proper place.
How to trust God with it, moment by moment.
Grief is painful.
It is gut-wrenching.
It is heavy.
And still—being entrusted with it is sacred.
Because when grief is carried with God, it becomes a vessel that holds love, hope, and eternal promise—all at once.

## Question

What has my grief been asking of me lately—and how might God be inviting me to hold it with both gratitude for the love that was given and purpose for how that love can still be carried forward?
If my grief were something entrusted to me rather than something happening to me, what might God be shaping in me through it—and how could that become a source of comfort or life for someone else?

## Prayer

God, I bring You my grief just as it is.
Not trimmed down.
Not explained away.
Not dressed up to look manageable.
I bring You the ache.
The absence.
The moments when memory feels like comfort and wound at the same time.
Thank You that You do not ask me to choose between sorrow and faith.
Thank You that You are present in both.
You are close to the brokenhearted.
You bind wounds that are too deep for words.
You strengthen me when grief weakens my knees and steals my breath.
I honor the love that created this grief.
I honor the life that mattered so deeply it left this mark on me.
I refuse to treat my sorrow as something shameful or inconvenient.
This grief is holy.
It exists because love existed.
And I thank You that love does not end at death.

Jesus, I thank You for Your resurrection.
Because You rose, grief does not get the final word.
Because You live, I live with hope—real hope, not
imagined comfort.
I hold tightly to the promise that one day You will wipe
away every tear.
That death will be undone.
That mourning and crying and pain will cease.
That what feels fractured now will be restored completely.
Until that day, teach me how to carry this grief with
purpose.
Not letting it crush me.
Not pretending it doesn't exist.
But allowing it to mature into compassion, depth, and
quiet strength.
Use the comfort You have given me
to comfort others who are walking this same road.
Let what I have endured become a place of connection,
not isolation.
Thank You for trusting me with this grief.
Thank You for walking with me as I learn how to live
alongside it.
Thank You that even here—especially here—You are at
work.
I celebrate the love that was.
I honor the pain that remains.
And I place my hope firmly in the resurrection to come.
I am held.
I am not alone.
And this story is not finished.
Amen

# Invitation Fifteen: Tending the Flame

There's a parable Jesus tells that has always felt sobering to me—not because it's cruel, but because it's honest.
In Matthew 25, Jesus speaks of ten young women who were all headed to the same celebration.
All invited.
All hopeful.
All carrying lamps.
Five of them were diligent.
Five of them were not.
Each one had oil. Each one had a flame at some point. But somewhere along the way, five of them grew weary, distracted, or careless. Scripture doesn't tell us exactly how it happened. It simply tells us the result: when the moment finally came, their lamps were dark.
And the truth that often feels uncomfortable—but necessary—is this:
the ones who had tended their oil could not give it away.
Not because they were selfish.
Not because they lacked compassion.
But because oil cannot be borrowed.
If I am prepared with just enough oil to keep my lamp burning until the celebration arrives, and I pour that oil into someone else's lamp, now neither of us is ready. Both lights go out. Both are left in the dark.
That's not generosity.
That's neglect—of myself and of the purpose I've been entrusted with.
And the same truth applies in reverse.

If I grow weary.
If I fall asleep spiritually.
If I let busyness, distraction, or exhaustion replace attentiveness.
If I stop tending my lamp and my flame goes out—
I cannot borrow the oil of someone else's transformation.
I cannot live on my friend's understanding of God.
I cannot rely on my neighbor's intimacy with Him.
I cannot coast on someone else's faithfulness.
Each of us is responsible for our own lamp.
That doesn't mean we walk alone.
It means we walk honestly.
The oil that fuels my flame comes from one place—and one place only.
The Source.
God Himself.
If I don't go to Him for replenishment, my light will go out.
And that won't be anyone else's fault. I won't be able to blame circumstances, seasons, exhaustion, or even grief.
Oil doesn't magically appear in the lamp.
I can have an entire vat of oil sitting in the corner of the room—but if I never pour it into my lamp, the flame still dies. Availability doesn't equal intimacy. Proximity doesn't equal participation.
And oil alone isn't enough.
I can have oil in my lamp, but if I never tend the wick—if I never strike the flame, protect it, nurture it—there is still no light.
Both matter.
Oil and flame.
Source and stewardship.
This is not about pressure.
It's about priority.
No matter how full my life gets.
No matter how tired I feel.
No matter how long the journey seems.

Tending the oil that fuels my light must remain central.
And here's the beautiful part: the more faithfully I tend my own lamp, the more visible the light becomes.
I can't light someone else's wick.
I can't pour oil into someone else's lamp.
I can't do their tending for them.
But I can shine.
And light has a way of drawing people in.
Like moths to a porch light on a summer night, people are drawn—not to effort, not to performance—but to real, steady illumination. And my deepest hope is not that others admire the light I carry, but that they realize they can have their own.
That they would look and say, I want that kind of light.
And then go to the Source themselves.
I want to live so connected to God that the oil never stops flowing—like an IV, a constant feed. Not frantic refilling. Not last-minute scrambling. But a steady, ongoing connection where my only responsibility is to remain attentive and tend what He supplies.
I want my lamp burning when the Bridegroom arrives.
Not because I was perfect.
But because I was faithful.
Because I stayed awake.
Because I kept returning to the Source.
Because I tended the flame I was given.
This is not about fear.
It's about readiness.
And readiness is an act of love.
Weariness doesn't always come from rebellion.
Sometimes it comes from overextension.
From giving without returning to be filled.
From tending everyone else's lamps while neglecting our own.

Distraction doesn't usually announce itself loudly.
It creeps in quietly—through busyness, responsibility,
noise, even good intentions—until attentiveness erodes
little by little.
Renewal begins the moment we stop pretending we're fine
and return to the Source with honesty. Not to prove
ourselves. Not to catch up. But to receive again what we
were never meant to manufacture.
The flame doesn't need theatrics.
It needs presence.

## A Question to Carry

Where have I been assuming oil will be there—without
intentionally returning to the Source to receive it?

## Prayer

God,
Teach me how to tend what You've entrusted to me.
Not with anxiety,
but with faithfulness.
When I grow tired, draw me back to You.
When I'm distracted, steady my attention.
When the flame feels small, remind me that You are the
Source—and You never run dry.
Help me stay awake.
Help me stay connected.
Help me tend the flame with joy.
May my readiness be an offering of love
when You arrive.
Amen

# Invitation Sixteen: Into Absolute Truth

There is a place we all pass through each day—
a thin threshold between sleep and waking.
Not fully unconscious.
Not fully alert.
It's where sounds blur, meaning shifts, and the mind fills in
gaps before the heart has time to discern. It's a vulnerable
space. And what we assume in that space can feel just as real
as what is true.
I know this place well.
I once slept in someone else's home—unfamiliar walls,
unfamiliar rhythms. In the middle of the night, I heard
sirens wailing and a dog whimpering, howling in distress.
My body responded before my mind could reason. My
heart raced. Something felt urgent. Dangerous.
Those were the facts as my sleeping mind understood
them.
But when morning came, the truth emerged.
There were no sirens.
No wounded animal.
No crisis unfolding in the dark.
It was only the wind—familiar to the homeowner, and
almost comforting to them as they sleep.
The facts formed one story.
The truth told another.
I've felt it again in that familiar jolt while sleeping—the
sensation of falling. The stomach drops. Muscles tense.
Every signal insists, You are not safe.
But I am.
The truth is, I'm still in the center of the bed.
I haven't moved.
There is nowhere to fall.
Facts can be convincing.
Feelings can be loud.
But neither are reliable narrators of truth.

Scripture gives us a framework for discernment—not denial:
"Finally, brothers and sisters,
whatever is true,
whatever is honest,
whatever is just,
whatever is pure,
whatever is lovely,
whatever is of good report,
if there is anything excellent or praiseworthy—
think about these things."
—Philippians 4:8
This passage doesn't tell us to ignore facts.
It tells us to filter them.
Facts are clues—not conclusions.
They can be misunderstood.
Misinterpreted.
Taken out of context.
You can make a deeply faulty—and even damaging—
decision based on facts alone.
Truth requires something more.
Truth requires clarity.
Perspective.
And often—relationship.
That's especially true when it comes to God Himself.
I can listen to other people's stories about Him.
I can consider their experiences.
Those facts matter.
But I cannot base my understanding of God on someone
else's relationship with Him.
Just as I don't decide who someone truly is based solely on
another person's opinion, I can't determine the nature of
God from secondhand accounts alone. At some point, I
have to show up myself.
I have to spend time with Him.
Listen.
Sit close.

Ask questions.
Pay attention.
I have to climb into His lap, so to speak, and allow Him to reveal who He is—personally, not theoretically.
Until I do that, I may have facts about God...
but I don't yet have truth.
And this principle doesn't stop with faith. It reaches into every area of life.
Facts and feelings shift.
Experiences vary.
Perceptions change.
But truth remains.
God's truth is unchanging.
It is found in His Word.
It is embodied in Jesus Himself.
There is no variation—no shadow of turning.
That kind of truth becomes a foundation—solid, weight-bearing. And from that foundation flows freedom. From freedom, righteousness. And from a life anchored there, others begin to notice.
Not because I'm persuasive.
Not because I'm flawless.
But because truth, when lived, has a gravity of its own.
People see freedom and want to know where it comes from.
They see steadiness and wonder how it's possible.
And they begin to seek—not my answers—but their own relationship with the Source.
That, for me, is a large part of my purpose.

To live with clarity.
With attentiveness.
With a heart firmly anchored.
Not ruled by half-formed conclusions.
Not led by fear in the night.
But grounded in truth—God's truth.
Because facts can change.
Feelings can lie.
But truth never does.
And learning to tell the difference
is how we move
from drifting and reacting
to living
with steadiness,
with discernment,
and with deep confidence
in Him.

### Reflective Question

Where have I been allowing facts, feelings, or secondhand experiences to shape my understanding—without personally seeking God's truth for myself in that place?

- What is one area of my life where I need to pause, filter what I'm sensing, and return to God to understand what is actually true?
- Where might God be inviting me to move beyond assumptions and into a deeper, personal knowing of His truth?

### A Prayer for Truth

God,
I want to know what is truly true.
Not just what feels convincing.
Not just what I've been told.

Not just what I've assumed in the dark.
I confess how easily I let facts and feelings speak louder
than You.
How quickly I draw conclusions before sitting with You
long enough to listen.
How often I react instead of discerning.
Teach me how to slow down.
How to filter what I see and hear through Your presence.
How to bring my questions to You without fear or
performance.
I don't want a borrowed understanding of You.
I don't want a secondhand faith.
I want to know You for myself.
Help me come close.
Help me stay long enough to recognize Your voice.
Help me trust that Your truth is steady—even when my
experience is not.
Anchor me where You are unchanging.
When facts shift, hold me steady.
When feelings rise and fall, remind me where my
foundation is.
I want my life to rest on what does not move.
I want the freedom that comes from truth.
I want the quiet confidence that grows from walking with
You, not just thinking about You.
Lead me into clarity.
Into discernment.
Into a deeper knowing of who You are.
And let the truth You place within me
become light for others—
not because I have answers,
but because I have learned to stay close to You.
Amen

# Invitation Seventeen: Finding the Center

Lately, I've been wondering as I listen to the noise all around me regarding the roles of men and women- the confusion, the rage, the justification, and the demands for retribution- God, what is YOUR desire for us, your creation? We know what we're seeing is brokenness. How can it be brought back into YOUR original intention?
I hear the stories—how men have dominated, how women have been mistreated, pushed down, overlooked, silenced. And it is frustrating. It is discouraging. And I know, without hesitation, that women being diminished by men is not the way God intended. We can see that clearly in the beginning —when God created humanity in His image and after His likeness. Male and female. Both bearing His reflection.
At the same time, I don't believe men should be villainized for stepping into roles of protection, responsibility, leadership, and wallowing in all the amazing qualities that God Himself put within men.
I don't believe strength itself is the problem. And I don't believe assigning blame—on either side—has brought us any closer to healing. What I keep sensing is that we've been pushed out of our God-intended design by a pendulum that swings too far one direction, then violently back the other way.
Instead of asking God, "Where is the balance? What was Your original intention?", we keep reacting—grabbing the weight, pulling harder, and letting it fly.
So I've been chewing on this. Sitting with it. Reading Scripture. Asking God to show me what He sees. These are the thoughts and understandings I'm coming to right now —not as final answers, but as a place I'm landing for the moment. And I trust He'll keep teaching me as I keep listening.

I keep coming back to Genesis 3. The serpent is crafty. He is subtle. He doesn't begin with flat-out rebellion—he begins with a question to stir doubt.

"Did God really say...?"

The woman answers him plainly. She repeats what God has said. There's no ignorance here. No confusion. She KNOWS God's loving instruction.

And then the serpent does what he's always done—he continues to stir doubt. He suggests that God might be withholding something good. That perhaps God cannot be fully trusted. That maybe they would be wiser if they chose for themselves.

And the text says this: "When the woman saw that the tree was good for food, and that it was a delight to the eyes, and that the tree was desirable to make one wise, she took from its fruit and ate; and she gave also to her husband WITH HER, and he ate." —Genesis 3:6

That phrase—with her—matters. They were together.This wasn't a private failure. It wasn't manipulation. It wasn't force. It was a shared moment of doubt. Together, they chose to decide for themselves rather than trust what God had said. Together, they stepped outside the balanced, loving order God had established.

And later, when God comes to them—not in rage, but in loving pursuit—He asks questions. "Where are you?" "What happened?" Not because He doesn't know. But because, sadly, relationship has fractured. Both man's relationship with God AND man's relationship with each other.

And when God speaks to the serpent, and then to the woman, and then to the man, I don't hear endorsement—I hear exposure.

To the woman, God says: "I will greatly multiply your pain in childbirth… Yet your desire will be for your husband, and he will rule over you." —Genesis 3:16

I don't read this as God saying, "I am now placing you under oppression, and I endorse it." I hear something else. I hear God naming what has just been unleashed. Because when trust with God breaks, trust between humans breaks too.

What had been partnership becomes tension. What had been harmony becomes struggle. What had been shared discernment becomes competing control.

This isn't a curse imposed from above—it's a description of the consequence of the choice. Not, "This is what I want." But, "This is what happens when relationship fractures." And that fracture didn't begin in marriage. It began in humanity.

This is where I think we've misunderstood both men and women for generations.

But as I sit with God, what He keeps showing me is this: Healing doesn't come from reversing the hierarchy. It comes from restoring the center.

Oppression isn't healed by reversing dominance.

Broken trust isn't healed by control.

And power struggles aren't healed by flipping who holds the weight. That's when I picture the pendulum.

People are standing in a circle.

Someone grabs the weight and pulls it as far as they can, letting it swing—knowing it will hit others.

Then someone else, now honestly hurt, grabs it and swings it the opposite way.

And people keep getting hurt. Because no one is asking where the pendulum was meant to rest.

When I crawl up into God's lap and ask Him what He sees, I don't sense Him pulling harder in either direction.

I sense Him pointing—quietly—to the center. To design. To order rooted in pure love. To interdependence.

Men and women were never meant to compete for rule. They were never meant to distrust one another. They were never meant to live in cycles of dominance and reaction.

They were meant to live with God—and therefore with each other—in trust.

This invitation isn't about husbands and wives. It's about humanity. About how men and women move through the world together—families, communities, leadership, work, and worship.

And in a world that is loud and confused—pulling the pendulum harder every generation—I'm finding that the most faithful thing to do is stop grabbing the weight.

When women have been suppressed, we've sometimes treated that suppression as divinely endorsed—rather than as evidence of a broken system God never intended.

And when that harm is recognized, the pendulum swings hard the other way—toward female dominance, superiority, and reversal of power "to make up for lost time".

Instead, step back. Sit with Scripture. Ask God what was always meant to be.

Because when the pendulum rests, the noise fades, the wounds begin to heal, and the balance we've been longing for quietly reappears.

## A Reflective Question

Where have I reacted to the noise and pain around me
instead of seeking God's center—and how might I have
unknowingly helped keep the pendulum swinging rather
than resting where He intended?
This question doesn't force guilt; it invites ownership,
discernment, and return.

## A Prayer of Responsibility, Clarity, and Restoration

God,
I come to You honestly—without defense, without excuses.
I acknowledge that I have lived inside this brokenness too.
I have absorbed the noise.
I have reacted to pain.
I have formed opinions shaped by hurt, history, and fear
rather than always by Your heart.
Forgive me for the ways I have contributed—knowingly or
unknowingly—to keeping the pendulum moving.
Forgive me for the times I have grabbed the weight
instead of stepping back to ask where You intended it to
rest.

Forgive me for mistaking the battle as one between men
and women, when the real battle has always been between
truth and deception.
Open my eyes to see what is actually happening.
Remind me that the enemy's goal has never been gender
—it has always been to fracture what bears Your image.
To divide what You designed for harmony.
To distort trust—first with You, and then with one another.
Teach me to see men as You see them.
Teach me to see women as You see them.
Not through tradition.
Not through reaction.
Not through wounds.
Restore in me the ability to honor rightly—
to honor strength without fear,
to honor tenderness without diminishing it,
to honor leadership without suspicion,
and partnership without competition.
Bring me back—back before the whispers of doubt,
back before mistrust entered,
back before power replaced love.
Let me live from the center You established—
where truth is clear,
where trust is possible,
and where Your design brings life instead of division.
I choose to stop grabbing the pendulum.
I choose to sit with You.
I choose to learn again.
And I ask You to heal what has been fractured—
in me,
between us,
and in the world You love.
Amen

# Invitation Eighteen: Soaking in What Has Been Stirred

Before we move forward, I want to pause again.
Not because we've run out of things to say—
but because what we've just walked through is not meant
to be rushed past.
Invitations Thirteen through Seventeen aren't merely
thoughts to consider. They are invitations to become—to
let God reshape the inner framework from which we live,
respond, interpret, forgive, discern, and love.
This is the kind of work that doesn't happen by skimming.
It happens by soaking.
We've been reminded that our bodies are not separate
from our spiritual lives—this sacred space is where the
Spirit of God dwells. We're learning to honor the body
with gratitude and balance, not shame or control.
We've stepped into grief—not as something to "get over,"
but as something holy to carry with God. We're learning
that grief can mature... and that pain can become a vessel
for compassion and purpose without ever diminishing
love.
We've been sobered by the call to tend the flame—to stay
connected to the Source, to remain honest, to resist
distraction, and to let readiness become an act of love
rather than fear.
We've been invited into absolute truth—to filter facts and
feelings through God's steady voice, and to refuse to build
our lives on half-formed conclusions, secondhand faith,
or assumptions made in the dark.
And we've stepped into the noise surrounding men and
women—and we've heard God pointing us toward the
center. Not dominance. Not reversal. Not blame. But
restoration. Interdependence. Design rooted in love. A
willingness to stop grabbing the pendulum and instead sit
with Scripture until we can see through His eyes.

Taken together, these are not small shifts.
These are paradigm shifts.
And if we don't pause here—if we don't let these truths
settle beneath the surface—then they can remain beautiful
words instead of becoming lived reality.
So this invitation is simply a holy pause.
A place to let what God is revealing move from
understanding...
into transformation.
Not by striving.
But by remaining.
Because when we see more through God's eyes, we
naturally begin to live differently.
We respond differently.
We speak differently.
We steward differently.
We forgive differently.
We honor differently.
We trust differently.
Not because we forced change—
but because our vision changed.
And vision changes everything.

# Questions to Sit With

- You don't have to answer all of these. Sit with the ones that feel quietly "alive." Let God choose what He wants to press gently on today.
- What has God been highlighting most strongly in Invitations 13–17—and what might He be inviting me to practice, not just understand?
- Where have I been living from disconnection—trying to manage life through effort, control, or self-protection —instead of remaining close to the Source?
- What is my body asking for right now—and how could I respond with reverence rather than frustration, guilt, or neglect?
- Where has grief been trying to overtake my life—or where have I tried to silence it—and what would it look like to let God teach me how to carry it faithfully?
- Where am I running low on oil—and what has been quietly draining me without replenishing me?
- In what area have facts, feelings, or assumptions been shaping my responses more than truth—and what would it look like to return to God for clarity there?
- Where am I tempted to grab the pendulum—reacting, defending, blaming, dominating, withdrawing—rather than sitting with God until I can see the center?
- If God is reshaping how I see the world, what might He be asking me to stop participating in—conversations, patterns, habits, mindsets—that keep me living from the old lens?
- What would "living from God's eyes" look like in one ordinary part of my day—my tone, my attention, my pace, my words, my relationships, my decisions?

## A Prayer of Soaking and Transformation

Father,
I pause here with You.
Not to gather more information,
but to let what You've been showing me sink deep enough
to change me.
I don't want these invitations to remain beautiful words.
I want them to become the inner framework I live from—
the lens I see through,
the foundation I stand on,
the posture I carry into the world.
Teach me to remain close.
Help me honor this body as sacred space—
not with obsession,
not with shame,
but with gratitude, wisdom, and joy.
Meet me in grief—
not asking me to rush healing,
not asking me to pretend I'm fine,
but tending what is tender until it no longer bleeds
uncontrollably.
Teach me how to carry love and sorrow together with
hope.
Keep my lamp burning.
Forgive me for the ways I've tried to live on fumes—
for tending everything except the flame You entrusted to
me.
Draw me back to the Source again and again,
until returning to You becomes my most natural rhythm.
Anchor me in truth.
When facts are loud and feelings surge,

steady me.
Teach me discernment.
Teach me to filter everything through Your presence,
and to build my life on what does not move.
And Father—heal what has been fractured in how we see
one another.
Open my eyes to recognize the real battle.
Not men against women.
Not people against people.
But deception against the image of God.
Deliver me from reaction.
Deliver me from the urge to grab the pendulum.
Teach me to sit with You until I can see the center—
Your design, Your heart, Your intention rooted in love.
Transform me as I soak.
Let Your truth settle into my bones,
into my instincts,
into my assumptions,
into my choices—
until my life naturally reflects You.
Not because I tried harder—
but because I stayed close.
I give You my pace.
I give You my vision.
I give You my heart.
Do Your quiet work in me.
And let it spill out as peace, steadiness, discernment,
tenderness, courage, and love
in the world around me.
I remain here with You.
I trust You with the process.
And I receive what only You can give.
Amen

# Invitation Nineteen: Staying Salty

Today I've been pondering salt.
Not metaphorically at first—just honestly. Its value. Its effect. The way it shows up quietly and yet changes everything it touches.
Salt has always mattered. Long before refrigeration, it preserved food. It kept things from decaying. It protected what would otherwise spoil. It was valuable enough to trade with, valuable enough to be fought over. Roman soldiers were sometimes paid with it. Salt wasn't decoration—it was necessity.
And then Jesus says something startling:
"You are the salt of the earth.
But if the salt loses its saltiness, how can it be made salty again?
It is no longer good for anything, except to be thrown out and trampled underfoot."
—Matthew 5:13
That sentence has been echoing in me.
If we are called salt, then salt isn't just something we use— it's something we are. And that has to shape how we think about how we live.
As surrendered believers—those who have accepted the sacrifice of Christ's blood and yielded our lives to Him—we are, in truth, the only authentic, pure, fully mineralized salt this world will ever know.
That's not pride.
That's responsibility.
The world doesn't encounter Christ directly—it encounters Him through His people. Through lives surrendered, hearts aligned, words seasoned, obedience lived out.
Which means it is absolutely critical—not just for me, but for the world around me—that I remain salty.
Last night, I was making vanilla pudding. Milk. Sugar. Cornstarch. Vanilla. Sweet, simple ingredients. And then— salt.
Just a pinch.

Salt tastes nothing like vanilla. It doesn't make the pudding
taste salty. But if you leave it out, you know immediately
that something is missing. The pudding doesn't taste as
much like vanilla without it.
Salt doesn't replace the flavor—it reveals it.
It makes things taste more like what they already are.
And then another thought came just as clearly.
If I had decided the pudding needed salt—and dumped in a
third of a cup—I wouldn't have improved it. I would have
destroyed it.
Too much salt ruins the recipe.
And that matters spiritually.
Because if I move through this world that desperately needs
salt—but I do so harshly, domineeringly, without grace or
respect—I'm no longer seasoning. I'm overwhelming.
I'm forcing cups and cups of salt onto people God is still
lovingly working with.
And that doesn't draw anyone toward truth.
It repels them.
God doesn't shout people into transformation.
He draws them—by His kindness.
And if I am meant to reflect His character, then my
saltiness must be grace-filled. Strong, yes—but gentle.
Clear, but kind. Present without being pushy.
Salt is powerful—but it works best in right measure.
Paul seems to echo this wisdom when he writes:
"Let your conversation be always full of grace, seasoned
with salt,
so that you may know how to answer everyone."
—Colossians 4:6
Seasoned.
Not dumped.
Not forced.

Salt is meant to enhance—not overpower.
And salt affects everything it comes into contact with.
If you've spent time near the coast, you know this. Salt hangs in the air. It settles invisibly. It adds minerals to the body—I'll walk barefoot in the ocean just to absorb them. It heals some things.
And yet—it corrodes others.
Metal rusts faster near saltwater. Cars driven on salted winter roads corrode more quickly. Salt preserves life and safety—but it also reveals what cannot withstand constant exposure.
Salt exposes.
Even in my yard, I see it. A simple salt-and-vinegar spray kills weeds in the cracks of a walking path. That's its purpose. But if I'm careless—if I drift off the path—it kills the flowers too.
Salt doesn't discriminate.
It requires wisdom.
Which brings me back again to Jesus' warning—not spoken in anger, but in clarity:
"Salt is good, but if it loses its saltiness, how can you make it salty again?"
—Mark 9:50
Salt that no longer does what salt does isn't evil—it's ineffective.
And salt that is used without love is destructive.
So now my reflection deepens.
If I lose my saltiness, it's not just that I feel disconnected.
It's that the world around me is deprived.
If I neglect my relationship with God...
if I stop crawling up into His lap...
if I drift from His Word...
if obedience becomes optional...
if I withhold Christ instead of sharing Him...
then I'm withholding salt.

And the dish doesn't taste like it was meant to.
But if I rush in without grace—
without kindness—
without patience—
I ruin the recipe God is still lovingly forming.
I don't ever want to be responsible for someone not getting
to taste of the Lord—either by neglect or by force.
I want to be faithful salt.
Salt that stays close to its Source.
Salt that hasn't been diluted.
Salt that hasn't been weaponized.
Salt that seasons conversations, preserves what's good,
resists decay, and reveals truth—with humility and love.
So my questions remain quiet—and weighty.
If I am salt...
am I present in the right measure?
am I seasoned with grace?
am I enhancing what God is already doing?
or am I overwhelming the very thing He's trying to bring
to fullness?
I don't think Jesus was calling us to overwhelm the world.
I think He was calling us to be faithful,
attentive,
and kind.
Because the world is hungry—
and it has no other salt.

## Questions to Sit With

Where might God be inviting me to remain faithfully salty
—present, pure, and attentive—without either withholding
myself through neglect or overwhelming others without
grace?
If you'd like a slightly different emphasis, here are two
quiet alternatives you could choose from:
- Am I staying close enough to God to be effective salt,
  and gentle enough to season the world around me in
  the way He intends?
- In what areas of my life do I need God's wisdom to help
  me know when to step forward with truth—and when to
  let grace do its slow, transforming work?

-

## A Prayer for Faithful Salt

God,
I come to You with open hands and an honest heart.
You have called me the salt of the earth,
and I feel the weight of that calling—not as burden,
but as trust.
I want to remain close to You,
because I know salt loses its savor when it drifts from its
source.
Draw me back again and again—
back to Your presence,
back to Your Word,
back to a life shaped by obedience and love.

Teach me how to be faithfully present in the world You
love. Help me neither to withhold myself through fear or
neglect,
nor to overwhelm others by forcing what only You can
grow.
Season my words with grace.
Measure my actions with wisdom.
Let kindness lead my truth,
just as Your kindness has always led me to You.
Guard my heart from hardness.
Keep me attentive, gentle, and strong.
Where decay threatens, help me preserve what is good.
Where truth is hidden, help me reveal it with care.
Where You are already at work, help me not interfere—but
join You.
I don't want to ruin the recipe You are patiently forming.
I want to enhance what You are doing,
to bring out the flavor of life You intended from the
beginning.
Make me salt that heals,
salt that preserves,
salt that draws rather than repels.
And when I am tired, remind me that this calling is not
carried alone.
Stay close, Lord.
Keep me close.
May my life help others taste and see
that You are good.
Amen

# Invitation Twenty: Waiting for the Bloom

Lately, I've been sitting with the weight—and the meaning
—of waiting.
There is something of deep significance that I have been
praying for for more than a decade now. Not a whim. Not a
passing desire. Something necessary. Something that
matters—not just to me, but beyond me.
And there are days when the waiting feels heavy.
Recently, one of my grandchildren was in the garden with
me. We were planting flower bulbs together—placing them
into the soil the day before the nighttime temperatures
were forecasted to drop into the teens and twenties.
As we worked, he shared his frustration. He has been
praying for the same thing I have. And he said, honestly
and quietly, that he was afraid God might never answer.
Afraid that the answer might not come at all.
So I paused and asked him a question.
"What are we planting these bulbs for?"
"So we can have flowers," he said.
I nodded. Then I asked another.
"What would happen if these bulbs bloomed today—
knowing how cold it's about to get?"
He thought for a moment, then said, "They would die."
Exactly.
If they bloomed too soon, they wouldn't survive the cold.
Not only would they fail in this season, but they could lose
their ability to bloom again at all. The very thing we want
—strong, lasting beauty—requires waiting. It requires
being hidden. It requires trust in timing.
So we placed the bulbs into the ground—not anxiously, not
wondering if they'll ever bloom—but with anticipation. We
trust the process. We trust the season. We trust that when
the right time comes, they will rise healthy and whole.
Prayer works the same way.

We place our requests before God now—often long before we see any evidence of change. And just like a winter garden, there are seasons when everything looks quiet. Bare. Still.

But beneath the surface, everything necessary is happening.

That's when I find myself thinking about Abraham.

God made Abraham a legitimate promise—one that seemed wildly unlikely at the time. A promise not meant to fulfill a private desire, but one that carried weight for generations. God's promise to Abraham was tied to His redemptive plan for the world.

Abraham built his life around that promise. He trusted God. He followed God. And yet—he grew tired of waiting. The fulfillment seemed delayed. The circumstances seemed impossible. And so Abraham did something deeply human: he tried to help God along.

In a sense, the flowers bloomed before the hard freeze. What came from that moment wasn't evil. It even looked reasonable at the time. But it wasn't God's timing, and it wasn't God's way. And the result—though it seemed workable in the moment—created consequences that reached far beyond that single decision.

And here's something I don't want to overlook.

Ishmael did not ask to be born into that situation.

He had no say in the impatience that shaped the circumstances of his arrival. Had he been born under the right conditions—under God's timing, within God's promise—I believe he would have been treasured by everyone involved. His mother's life would have unfolded differently. His future would have been shaped by belonging instead of displacement.

I believe Isaac's family and Ishmael's family could have walked together in beauty.

Instead, Ishmael became a son who was sent away rather than welcomed, a child who bore the weight of decisions he did not make.

The conflict that followed was not born from his existence
—it was born from impatience.
Thousands of years later, the ripple effects remain.
God remained faithful to His promise.
But human urgency complicated the story.
That reality humbles me.
Because it reminds me that when I try to force what God
has promised—when I step in out of fear, anxiety, or
discouragement—I don't just risk complicating my own life.
I may unintentionally affect others who never chose that
path.
We are not good at doing God's work for Him.
But we are invited to do God's work with Him.
With His wisdom.
With His power.
In His timing.
Waiting isn't passive. It's participatory. It's choosing trust
over control. It's resisting the urge to force blooms that
cannot yet survive the season.
Just because I don't see God's hand moving doesn't mean
He isn't at work. With bulbs beneath the soil, everything
required for future beauty is already underway.
Roots are forming.
Strength is developing.
Protection is in place.
So I'm choosing to wait with anticipation—not anxiety.
With hope—not fear.
With trust—not resignation.
I don't want to create Ishmaels in my impatience.
I want to receive Isaacs in God's time.
I may not see the work right now.
But I know the One who promised.
And when the season is right,
the bloom will come—
strong enough to last,
gentle enough to bless,
and perfectly timed to give Him glory.

## A Question to Ponder

Where am I most tempted to "help God along" right now
—and what would it look like, in that very place, to trust
His timing without going passive... to keep planting,
watering, and obeying, while leaving the blooming entirely
in His hands?

## A Prayer of Patient Anticipation

Father,
You see the place in me that gets tired of winter.
You see the years I've been praying.
You see the significance of what I'm asking for—how it's
not a passing whim, but something
weighty and necessary. And You also see the days when the
waiting feels heavy, when silence feels like absence, and
when my heart wonders if anything is happening at all.
So I come to You honestly.
Teach me how to wait with faith instead of fear.
Teach me how to hope without trying to control.
Teach me how to plant and trust the soil at the same time.
Lord, forgive me for the ways I've tried to force blooms
before the season was ready.
Forgive me for the moments I've stepped in out of
anxiety, trying to secure what You promised rather than
resting in the One who promised.
I do not want to complicate what You are writing.
I do not want to create consequences out of urgency.
I do not want to birth "solutions" that look workable but
carry grief for people who never chose them.

.

Give me humility—real humility.
The kind that stays close to You.
The kind that listens more than it rushes.
The kind that obeys what You've asked of me today and leaves tomorrow's unfolding to You.
And Father, I lift up the ones who get caught in the wake of other people's impatience—the Ishmaels of this world.
Those who carry weight they didn't choose. Those who have been displaced, overlooked, or made to feel like an unwanted outcome.You are the God who sees.
You are the God who provides.
You are the God who redeems what humans complicate.
So I ask You: Redeem. Restore. Heal. Gather.
Do what only You can do.
As I wait, keep my heart soft.
Keep my spirit steady.
Keep my hands faithful.
Let my waiting be participatory—full of prayer, full of trust, full of obedience—without grasping, forcing, or panicking
When I can't see what You're doing beneath the surface, remind me: Roots are forming. Strength is developing.
Protection is in place.
And when the season is right—when the bloom can survive, when it can bless, when it can endure—bring it forth in a way that makes it unmistakably Yours.
I trust You with the timing.
I trust You with the process.
I trust You with the promise.
And I choose, today, to wait with anticipation.
Amen

# Invitation Twenty-One: What Is Leavening My Life

Lately, my thoughts have been resting on something simple—and alive.
Leaven.
Yeast.
Sourdough starter.
Anyone who knows me knows how much I love sourdough. There's always a small jar on my counter—quietly bubbling, being fed, tended, watched. I pull a bit off, make something nourishing, then feed what remains so it can keep living.
And the more I work with it, the more I notice how much Scripture has been quietly teaching me through this living thing.
There's a clear difference between lab-created yeast and wild yeast.
With commercial yeast, I can bake a loaf in three or four hours. It's efficient. Predictable. Fast.
But sourdough—wild yeast—takes time. Eight, ten, twelve hours. Sometimes longer. And yet the bread it makes is different altogether. More flavorful. More nourishing. Better texture. Better structure. More depth.
And something else fascinates me.
The wild yeast gathered in Alaska is different from the wild yeast in San Francisco. And both are different from the yeast I gather right where I live. Flour and water capture what's already in the air. The environment shapes what grows. What's living around me becomes what's living within the dough.
Scripture says,
"A little leaven leavens the whole lump."
—1 Corinthians 5:6
That sentence is both sobering and powerful.
Leaven doesn't stay contained.
Because it's alive, it spreads.
It permeates everything it touches.

"Sometimes Scripture uses leaven as a warning—about sin, hypocrisy, false teaching. Other times, it uses the same image to describe something beautiful and holy.
Jesus tells a parable that reframes leaven entirely:
The kingdom of heaven is like leaven, which a woman took and hid in three measures of flour until it was all leavened."
—Matthew 13:33
That matters.
The same quality that makes leaven dangerous in the wrong context—its ability to spread quietly and completely—is the very thing that makes it powerful in God's hands.
The kingdom of God does not arrive loudly.
It does not dominate by force.
It begins small.
Hidden.
Almost unnoticed.
And then it works its way through everything.
Jesus is saying: this is how My kingdom moves.
A small beginning.
A living presence.
A quiet permeation that eventually transforms the whole.
And suddenly, leaven becomes an invitation—not just a warning.
Because if a little leaven leavens the whole lump, then what God places alive within me—His Spirit, His truth, His Word—has the power to shape everything I touch.
When I bake a loaf of bread, it might be a large, heavy mass of dough—but it only takes a small amount of starter to make the whole thing rise. That tiny portion expands everything. It even forces change. If I don't score the loaf before baking, it will tear itself open under the pressure of growth.

Life works the same way.
What is alive in me will expand.
What I carry will be felt.
What I nurture will eventually be seen.
Leaven is alive. And when it's placed in the right environment, it multiplies quickly.
I can slow it down by putting it in the refrigerator—limiting the conditions that help it grow. Or I can place it somewhere warm, safe, and womb-like, and it will flourish rapidly.
So the question becomes deeply personal.
What am I allowing to live in me?
What environment am I creating for it to grow?
What am I feeding?
Because I don't get to manufacture "lab yeast" inside my soul. What grows in me is gathered—wild—formed by what I expose myself to, what I sit with, what I consume, what I allow access to my thoughts and heart.
If what is alive in me is God's truth—His Word, His presence, His Spirit—then that life will leaven everything I touch: my home, my family, my friendships, my conversations, my worship, my daily interactions.
This is how the kingdom spreads.
Not through pressure.
Not through performance.
But through presence.

But if what is alive in me is bitterness, fear, hypocrisy,
deception, or wounded patterns left untended—those too
will spread. They will shape the whole loaf.
The principle doesn't change.
Only the leaven does.
That's why Scripture urges discernment—not fear.
Because whatever is alive in me will not remain private.
It will expand.
It will permeate.
It will affect others.
So this invitation is not about control.
It's about attentiveness.
About asking, honestly and gently:
What is leavening my life?
Because I want what is alive in me to be life-giving.
I want what is growing in me to nourish.
I want the quiet influence I carry to be the kingdom at
work—patient, pure, and powerful.
Just like sourdough.
I don't leave my starter unattended for long.
I notice when it's weak.
I remove what's old.
I give it what it needs to stay healthy and alive.
I want to tend my inner life with the same care.
Because a little leaven leavens the whole lump.
And I want the leaven in me to be God's—
alive, holy, and quietly transforming everything it touches.

**A Question to Sit With**

If the quiet, unseen things shaping my thoughts, reactions,
and tone were allowed to fully rise—
what kind of "loaf" would my life become,
and would I recognize the leaven at work as God's
kingdom...
or something else I've been feeding without noticing?

**Prayer**

Father...
this one makes me slow down.
Because I know You're not asking this to shame me—
You're asking because You care about what's growing in
me.
So I'm bringing myself to You just as I am.
Not cleaned up.
Not edited.
Just honest.
I don't want to pretend that everything shaping me is holy.
Some of it is good and alive and from You—
and some of it has crept in quietly through tiredness, hurt,
fear, distraction, or habit.
And I don't always notice right away.
I don't always realize what I've been feeding
until I see what's rising.
So would You help me see?
Gently.
Clearly.

Show me what's alive in me right now.
What's being nurtured by my attention.
What's being strengthened by my choices—
even the small, daily ones.
If there's anything in me that isn't from You,
I don't want to ignore it or panic over it.
I just want to bring it into the light with You
and let You help me tend it rightly—or let it go.
And if what's growing is from You,
if Your Spirit is quietly leavening my life,
then help me protect that.
Feed that.
Give it room to rise.
I want what spreads from me
to nourish, not deplete.
To bring life, not tension.
To feel like Your kingdom moving quietly through
ordinary places.
I trust You with this work.
I trust You to show me what needs care
and what needs removing.
I'm here.
I'm paying attention.
And I'm letting You tend what's growing in me.
Amen

# Invitation Twenty-Two: When the Ground Shakes

There are moments in Scripture that feel almost unbearable to sit with—not because they are unclear, but because they are so costly.

Acts 16 is one of those moments for me.

Paul and Silas were not merely arrested. They were tortured. Roman torture was intentional, brutal, and degrading—designed to strip skin from flesh, to expose what should never be exposed, to break both body and spirit. They were beaten, bound, and forced into stocks engineered to cause prolonged agony. Their wounds were open. The floor beneath them was stone and dirt. Every breath would have hurt. Every shift of weight would have torn skin again.

It was dark. It was filthy. It smelled of death.

And in that place—when most people would have been cursing their captors, or begging for relief, or wishing for death—they sang.

They worshiped.

Not because the pain wasn't real.

Not because God had explained Himself.

Not because suffering is somehow holy in itself.

But because they trusted Him in it.

Then the ground began to shake.

Not a gentle tremor. Not a symbolic moment. Chains snapped. Doors flew open. The foundations themselves were disturbed. Everything about the scene suggests escape—miraculous, undeniable escape.

Anyone would have run.

And no one would have blamed them.

But they didn't.

The jailer—the same man responsible for guarding them, likely involved in their mistreatment—woke to the sight of open doors. In Roman law, a lost prisoner meant a lost life. He prepared to kill himself rather than face execution.
And from the darkness came a voice.
"Don't harm yourself. We are all here."
They stayed.
And in that moment, something shifted. The earthquake had not come to free Paul and Silas from the prison. It came to free the jailer from despair. That night, the man who had bound them washed their wounds. The man who had overseen their suffering heard the gospel. His entire household believed. An entire family stepped into eternal freedom—because two battered men chose faithfulness over flight.
That story has stayed with me—not because it glorifies suffering, but because it reveals something deeper.
Sometimes God shakes the foundations beneath us not to remove us from the discomfort, but because someone else's freedom is bound up in our response.
And that is a hard truth to hold.
But here is something that must be said just as clearly:
God does not call His children to remain in abuse.
Faithfulness is not the same as staying in harm.
Endurance is not the same as enduring violation.
Submission is not the same as surrendering safety.
God does not ask us to sacrifice our dignity, our bodies, or our lives to prove devotion. Scripture affirms wisdom, protection, and the preservation of life. Jesus Himself stepped away from those who sought to harm Him.
Walking away from abuse can be an act of obedience.

What God does call us to—even when separation is necessary—is Christlikeness.
There is a godly way to stand up and walk away.
A way to set boundaries without retaliation.
A way to leave without becoming hardened or cruel.
A way to refuse harm without mirroring it.
Paul and Silas were not enduring abuse because suffering itself was holy. They were faithful within circumstances they did not choose—and when God created an opening, they responded with discernment rather than self-protection alone.
In the same way, when we must walk away from harm, we are still invited to let God shape how we leave. Not to remain silent. Not to tolerate evil. But to remain anchored—so that even our departure bears witness to truth.
That distinction matters.
Because often, what God is forming in us during the shaking is not just about our comfort, but about our character.
What if the moment when escape presents itself is not a test of our courage—but a test of our vision?
What if we could run... but God is asking us to remain present just long enough for someone else to encounter freedom?
What if we are tempted to compromise, to take the quickest way out, to do what is understandable but less than faithful—and instead, God is inviting us to keep producing the fruit of the Spirit right there in the pressure?
Not pretending the pain isn't real.
Not minimizing the cost.
But choosing worship over bitterness.
Trust over control.
Faithfulness over fear.

Sometimes, the shaking is not punishment.
Sometimes, it is preparation.
Sometimes, it is mercy for someone else.
And sometimes, the greatest miracle is not the open door—
but the heart that changes because we didn't run.


**A Question to Sit With**

Where is the ground shaking in my life right now—and
how might God be inviting me to remain faithful in how I
respond, whether that means staying, setting boundaries, or
walking away, so that Christ is still clearly seen through me?

**A Prayer**
God,
I bring You the places in my life that feel shaken—
the moments where the pressure is real,
the pain is undeniable,
and the way forward feels unclear.
I do not pretend that harm is holy.
I do not confuse faithfulness with self-abandonment.
I trust You as a God who protects, who sees, who cares for
the vulnerable
Teach me how to walk in wisdom.
How to discern when to stay, and when to step away.
How to set boundaries without hatred.
How to leave without retaliation.
How to remain Christlike even when I cannot remain
present.
And in the places where You ask me to stay—
where faithfulness costs something—
give me the strength to worship without denial,
to trust without bitterness,
to love without fear.
If You are shaking the ground beneath me,
help me see beyond my own relief.
Help me recognize where You may be working freedom
for someone else.
I choose faithfulness over flight.
Truth over reaction.
Trust over control.
Form in me the kind of life
that makes Your goodness visible—
whether I am staying,
or walking away,
or standing still in the dark.
I trust You with the outcome.
I trust You with my safety.
I trust You with the work You are doing—
in me, and beyond me.
Amen

# Invitation Twenty-Three: A Seat at the King's Table

There are some moments in Scripture that unfold quietly—but they change everything.

Second Samuel 4:4 is one of those moments.

Jonathan, the son of King Saul, had a young son named Mephibosheth. He was five years old when the news arrived from Jezreel that both his father, Jonathan, and his grandfather, Saul, had been killed in battle. When his nurse heard the report, she panicked. She picked him up and fled—running for safety, running from danger, running from what she feared would come next.

But in the haste, she fell.

And in that single moment—one slip, one accident—Mephibosheth lost the use of both of his legs.

He didn't do anything wrong.

He didn't make a bad decision.

He wasn't being punished.

His life was altered by something that happened to him. From that day forward, his story would be shaped by limitation—by how he moved through the world, how others perceived him, and how vulnerable he was within it.

And there was more.

Mephibosheth wasn't just injured—he was also dangerous by association.

He was the grandson of the former king. In that culture, the descendants of a deposed king were liabilities. Threats. Loose ends. They were often eliminated to prevent future rebellion. Mephibosheth would have known this. So he lived hidden—out of sight, out of reach, surviving but not thriving. Alive, but not free. Existing in a place where nothing really grows.

Then something extraordinary happens.

David becomes king.

And instead of securing his power through elimination, David remembers covenant.

Years earlier, David and Jonathan—young men then—had formed one of the most profound friendships recorded in Scripture.

God had knit their hearts together. They made promises to one another. They exchanged garments, symbolizing an exchange of identity, authority, and provision. Jonathan, the king's son, essentially said to David: what is mine is yours—my possessions, my influence, my future.
Now Jonathan is gone.
But David has not forgotten.
So he asks a question that changes Mephibosheth's life: "Is there anyone still left of the house of Saul, that I may show him kindness for Jonathan's sake?"
Not someone worthy.
Not someone impressive.
Not someone useful.
Just—anyone.
And they find Mephibosheth.
When Mephibosheth is summoned to the king, fear would have been unavoidable. Everything in his experience would have told him this summons meant judgment. Removal. Death. Yet he comes anyway. And David's first words to him are not accusation or suspicion, but reassurance: "Do not be afraid."
That matters.
Because grace never arrives carrying fear.
It quiets the fear that's already there.
David restores to Mephibosheth all the land that belonged to Saul. He gives him provision. Protection. And then something even more unthinkable:
He invites him to eat at the king's table—for the rest of his life.
Not as a guest.
Not as a charity case.
But as a son.
Mephibosheth remains lame. His condition doesn't suddenly disappear. But his position changes completely. His weakness is still real—but it no longer defines his worth. At the king's table, his brokenness is covered. His identity is rewritten. He belongs.

And this is where the story reaches into my own life.
Because this is exactly what Christ has done for me.
I did not earn a seat at the King's table.
I did not fix myself first.
I did not arrive strong, whole, or impressive.
I was broken.
I was hiding.
I was an enemy by nature.
And yet—because of Jesus—
I was invited.
Not for a single meal.
Not temporarily.
But permanently.
Scripture tells me that I am already seated with Christ in heavenly places—not after I'm healed, not after I'm polished, not after I'm made presentable. As I am. The healing happens at the table. The restoration happens in relationship.
Like Mephibosheth, I had a choice.
I could run—assuming judgment.
Or I could come—trusting the King.
And when I came, I discovered that grace didn't deny my condition—it covered it. My identity shifted from enemy to child. From hidden to known. From surviving to belonging.
That changes everything.
Because when I live as someone hiding in fear and brokenness, I have very little to offer the world around me.
But when I live as someone seated at the King's table—secure, provided for, loved—I carry the abundance of the Kingdom with me. And there is no limit to those resources.
I never want to forget this.
I never want to forget that I am here by covenant, not merit.
By grace, not worthiness.
By invitation, not entitlement.
And neither is anyone else.

## A Question to Sit With

Where in my life am I still living as though I am hiding from the King—rather than receiving the grace that has already invited me to sit at His table as His child?

## Prayer

Father...
I'm coming to You just as I am today.
Not trying to sound right.
Not trying to explain myself well.
Just bringing what's real.
I'm aware of how often I still live like I'm on the outside—
like I need to earn my way in,
like I need to fix myself before I'm allowed to come close.
And I know that isn't how You are.
But sometimes my fear speaks louder than truth.
So I'm sitting here with You now,
letting You remind me again
that I've already been invited.
That You didn't call me because I was strong or put-together.
You called me because You love me.
Thank You for keeping covenant when I forget.
Thank You for remembering me when I've been hiding.
Thank You for calling my name instead of pointing out my weakness.
I don't want to live like someone bracing for rejection anymore.
I don't want to keep expecting judgment where You're offering kindness.

I want to trust You enough to stay at the table.
Teach me how to receive—
not rush,
not minimize,
not push away what feels too generous.
Help me live from belonging instead of fear.
From security instead of scarcity.
From gratitude instead of shame.
Thank You that I don't have to clean myself up to be with
You.
Thank You that healing happens here—
in closeness,
in relationship,
in being seen and still loved.
I want to live like someone who knows they're Your child.
Not hiding.
Not shrinking.
Not apologizing for taking up space at the table.
Let the way I live reflect the abundance of Your Kingdom—
not because I earned it,
but because You are faithful
and You chose me.
I'm here.
I'm staying.
And I trust You with the rest.
Amen

# Invitation Twenty-Four: Staying With What You're Doing

Before I move on, I want to stay here a minute.
Not because I don't know what's next—
but because I don't want to hurry past what You're already
doing.
These last invitations haven't felt loud or dramatic.
They've felt slow.
Deep.
Like You've been working under the surface—
touching places that don't change overnight,
but shape everything that follows.
You've been teaching me how to wait without trying to fix
the waiting.
How to trust that what's hidden isn't forgotten.
That just because something hasn't bloomed yet
doesn't mean it isn't alive.
You've been drawing my attention to what is active within
me—
what I'm feeding,
what I'm giving room to grow,
what kind of leaven I'm carrying into every room I walk
into.
Because whatever is alive in me
won't stay contained—it will spread.

You've been showing me that worship doesn't disappear
when things hurt.
That sometimes praise isn't about relief,
but about staying aligned when the ground is shaking.
That obedience in those moments
might not be about getting me out—
but about freeing someone else.
You've also been gentle and clear with me—
that You don't ask me to remain in harm.
That walking away can still be holy.
That there is a way to leave without becoming hard,
to set boundaries without losing love,
to stand up without striking back.
And then You brought me back to the table again.
Not as someone who finally earned her place—
but as someone welcomed because covenant was kept.
You reminded me that I don't heal before I come close.
I heal because I'm close.
Taken together, I can feel it.
You're not asking me to do more.
You're inviting me to stay.
To let waiting soften me instead of making me anxious.
To guard what I'm allowing to shape me.
To keep choosing You when the easy exit appears.
To live from belonging, not fear.
So this is a pause—not to evaluate,
but to consent.
To say yes again.
To let You keep working.
To allow these truths to settle deeper
until they don't just sound right—
they feel natural.
I don't want to move on too quickly.
I don't want this to pass through me.
I want it to become how I live.

**Questions to Sit With Gently**

Not to answer all at once.
Not to solve.
Just to notice.
Where do I feel God inviting me to wait instead of act—
and what fear rises when I imagine trusting His timing
there?
What is currently being given space to grow within me, and
is it something I want shaping my life and the lives around
me?
Where am I being asked to keep responding with
Christlikeness—not to stay stuck, but to stay true?
In what ways am I still living like someone outside the table
instead of someone already welcomed?
What would it look like to let God keep working in these
areas without rushing toward resolution?

## A Short Return Prayer

Father...
I'm here.
I'm not trying to figure anything out right now.
I just want to stay close.
I don't want to rush what You're doing in me.
I don't want to skim past it or turn it into something neat
and finished.
I trust You with the pace.
I trust You with the pressure.
I trust You with the places that still feel unfinished.
I'm letting You keep working—
in my waiting,
in what I'm allowing to grow,
in how I respond when things are hard,
in how I hold my ground without hardening my heart.
I don't need to prove anything to You.
I don't need to clean myself up.
I'm just here—
leaning in,
listening,
letting You shape what needs shaping.
Stay with me while You do it.
I'm not going anywhere.
Amen

# Invitation Twenty-Five: To Carry God's Aroma

Lately, I've been paying attention to aroma.
I love waking up to the smell of coffee—how it moves
through the house before I ever see the cup. It doesn't
announce itself. It doesn't explain itself. It simply is. And
somehow, that aroma invites me into the day before I've
even decided what the day will hold.
Incense works differently—but just as deliberately.
When I blend resins, woods, and herbs and place them
over heat, nothing happens accidentally. The aroma isn't
the goal in itself. The aroma is the result of something
being offered—something placed intentionally and
allowed to rise.
That's the picture Scripture gives us.
David prayed,
"May my prayer be set before You like incense."
Not as decoration.
Not as atmosphere.
But as offering.
Throughout Scripture, incense was never about scent for
scent's sake. It was tied to prayer, surrender, intercession,
and worship. It rose because something was being given—
something costly, intentional, and reverent.
After the flood, Noah offered sacrifice, and Scripture says
the Lord received it as a pleasing aroma.
When Christ offered Himself, Paul tells us His life and
death were a fragrant offering to God.
And now, as someone who belongs to Christ, I'm told that
my life carries His aroma.
That's humbling.
Because aroma doesn't come from performance.
It comes from proximity.

And here's where this gets deeply personal for me.
For years, I've made my own fragrance. Slowly. Thoughtfully. It's not loud, but it's distinctive. And people notice. A bank teller pauses mid-transaction. Someone stops me in the grocery store. I've even had friends call and say, "You were just in that store, weren't you?" And when I ask how they know, they laugh and say, "I smelled you before I saw you. You're the only one who smells like that."
It's become something sweet and almost humorous. People recognize me by what lingers after I've passed through.
They'll hug me and hold on for a second longer and say, "You always smell so good." And what they're responding to isn't effort. It's consistency. It's something I've lived with long enough that it's become part of me.
And that's what I want my life with God to be like.
I don't want my faith to be something I explain well.
I want it to be something I carry.
I want my prayers—my honest, daily, sometimes messy conversations with God—to rise like incense. Not dramatic. Not performative. Just faithfully offered.
And I want the result of that life of prayer, surrender, and obedience to be the aroma of Christ.
Because Scripture is clear: I am carrying an aroma whether I intend to or not.
Paul says we are the fragrance of Christ to God—and to the world. And that same aroma will be received differently. Some will lean in. Some will recoil. The difference isn't the aroma. It's the heart of the one breathing it in.

Just like coffee.
Just like incense.
Just like Christ Himself.
So this invitation isn't about trying to be pleasant to
everyone.
It's about staying close enough to God that my life
naturally reflects Him.
When my prayers rise honestly.
When my desires are laid down humbly.
When I return to Him again and again instead of drifting.
Something happens that I don't have to manufacture.
I carry Him.
Into rooms.
Into conversations.
Into ordinary moments.
And whether someone is drawn or offended, my posture
stays the same: humility, faithfulness, kindness, and trust.
Because aroma doesn't need permission to travel.

### A Reflective Question

As I move through my daily life, what is rising from me—
and am I tending my relationship with God deeply enough
that what lingers after I leave is the aroma of Christ rather
than the residue of fear, striving, or self-protection?

## A Lap Prayer

Father...
I'm here again, tucked in close, listening.
I keep thinking about how incense only rises when
something is offered. And I'm realizing how much I want
my prayers—my real prayers, not polished ones—to rise to
You like that.
Not to create an atmosphere.
Not to feel spiritual.
But because I'm giving You my life again today.
If there's anything in me that's been feeding the wrong
things—fear, control, old wounds—I don't want to fix it
myself. I just want to bring it to You and let You change
what's rising from my life.
Teach me how to stay close enough to You that Your
presence clings to me naturally.
Teach me how to pray honestly and live surrendered
without trying to manage the outcome.
And when people are drawn—thank You.
When they turn away—help me not to shrink or harden.
Help me keep loving and trusting You with what I can't
control.
I don't want to announce You everywhere I go.
I want to carry You.
So I'm staying right here for a moment longer—letting my
prayers rise, letting You shape what follows me into the
world.
I love You.
I'm Yours.
And being near You is enough.
Amen

# Invitation Twenty-Six: The Quiet Undercurrent of Joy

Lately, I've been sitting with the difference between happiness and joy—and the more I sit with it, the clearer that difference becomes.
Happiness is something I can influence.
I can create it for a moment.
I can chase it.
I can manufacture a temporary sense of satisfaction.
Positive thinking.
Affirmations.
Achievements.
Goals met.
Dreams realized.
All of those can bring a high.
All of them can feel good.
And none of them can produce lasting joy.
Because joy is not something I produce.
Joy is something that grows.
Joy is a fruit of the Spirit.
Which means it is supernatural.
It is not emotional optimism.
It is not denial.
It is not pretending everything is fine.
It is the quiet, steady result of being connected to the vine.
I can hype myself into happiness.
I can distract myself into feeling better.
I can even accomplish everything I've set my heart on in this world—and still find that something deeper is missing.

Because joy does not come from fulfilled dreams.
It comes from a fulfilled connection.
Scripture tells me that since I've been justified by faith, I now stand in grace—and from that place, something entirely different is formed. Not just relief. Not just peace. But joy that remains even when suffering enters the story. Paul says we rejoice not only in hope, but even in suffering—not because suffering is good, but because of what God does through it. Endurance. Character. Hope. And hope that does not disappoint, because God's love has already been poured into my heart through the Holy Spirit.
Happiness could never do that.
Joy doesn't fluctuate the way emotions do.
It doesn't disappear when circumstances turn.
It runs underneath everything—like an undercurrent—steady and present, whether the surface is calm or stormy.
Jesus said there would be sorrow.
He didn't deny it.
He didn't minimize it.
But He also said joy would remain.
A joy no one could take.
That matters to me.
Because I don't want a life that collapses when happiness fades.

I want a joy that stays.
Scripture says God places more joy in my heart than others experience even when their lives overflow with abundance. That tells me joy is not about having more—it's about being rooted.
Jesus said He spoke His words so that His joy would be in me, and that my joy would be full. Not partial. Not fragile. Full.
And that fullness doesn't come from effort.
It comes from remaining.
I think about the vines in my yard.
Even when one branch looks strained or weather-worn, as long as it's connected, life is still flowing. Fruit still forms— quietly, faithfully.
But once a branch is severed, fruit is impossible.
Joy works the same way.
If I disconnect—if I drift from God's presence, neglect His Word, stop returning honestly—I don't lose salvation, but I do lose vitality. Fruit withers when connection weakens.
But when I remain—when I remember that Christ is in me and I am in Him—joy stays, even when happiness doesn't.
And here's something God has been gently showing me too:
Joy is always present—but expression is a choice.
I don't have to feel joyful to walk in joy.
I don't have to deny pain to express hope.
I don't have to ignore frustration to choose perspective.
Sometimes joy needs my participation.
Not pretending.
Not bypassing.
But choosing to let joy speak louder than frustration.

There are moments when I have to say,
"God, this hurts. This is hard. This is not what I wanted."
And then I ask Him something very specific:
"Would You please let me see this through Your eyes?"
I call it putting on God-goggles.
I'm not asking Him to erase the pain.
I'm asking Him to frame it.
To show me what I can't yet see.
To remind me where this story is headed.
When I do that, joy rises—not because the circumstance
changes, but because my perspective does.
Scripture tells me to rejoice in hope, to be patient in
tribulation, to be constant in prayer. That tells me joy isn't
passive—it's responsive. It's choosing to anchor myself in
what is already true.
Hard things still happen.
Pain still exists.
Grief still matters.
But hope is still alive.
The outcome is already secure.
The work is already done.
We are not waiting to win.
We are walking out a victory that's already been won.
That's why joy can remain.
Not because life is easy.
But because Christ is faithful.
Most days are happy.
But all days can be joyful.
And I want to live from that place—rooted, connected,
honest, and steady—where joy isn't something I chase, but
something that quietly grows because His life is flowing
through mine.

## A Reflective Question

When circumstances feel heavy or happiness fades, what
would change if I stopped trying to produce joy and
instead returned—again—to remaining connected, trusting
the Holy Spirit to do the work only He can do in me?

## A Lap Prayer

God...
I'm here again—quiet, close, and honest.
I can admit it now: I've tried to think my way into joy
before. I've tried to stay positive. I've tried to muscle
through. And You keep gently reminding me that joy isn't
something I create—it's something You grow.
Help me stay connected.
Help me stop striving.
Help me remember that joy doesn't disappear just because
happiness does.
When life hurts, let me see through Your eyes.
When frustration rises, steady me with hope.
When I don't understand what You're doing, remind me
that the ending is already secure.
Teach me how to express joy without denying pain.
Teach me how to rejoice without pretending.
Teach me how to live from the undercurrent instead of
reacting to the surface
I trust You to grow what I cannot manufacture.
I trust You with the fruit.
I'm staying right here.
Amen

# Invitation Twenty-Seven: Whose Approval Am I Living For?

This invitation didn't come from theory.
It came from practice.
Recently, I stepped into spaces I intentionally avoided for years—social platforms, public visibility, exposure. Not because I suddenly wanted attention, but because I'm building something that needs it.
I've worked physically for my income my entire adult life. And while I'm still strong and capable, I'm also wise enough to think about sustainability. About the years ahead. About building streams of income that don't require my body to carry all the weight.
And the truth is, if I want to build businesses that can support me without constant physical labor, exposure matters. People have to find what I'm offering. They have to decide whether it's valuable to them. That's not ego— that's economics. That's stewardship.
But stepping into visibility has a way of quietly testing the heart.
Because the line between offering something and seeking approval can blur faster than we realize.
Scripture names that tension without shame.
Paul says we've been approved by God and entrusted with the gospel—and because of that, we speak not to please people, but to please God, who examines our hearts.
That verse matters to me right now.
Because it reminds me that success, exposure, and even affirmation are not evil—but they are not neutral either.

They reveal what I'm anchoring myself to.
I would love for my books to be well received.
I would love for my work to support my life.
I would love to do meaningful, creative work without exhausting my body every day.
But I don't want ease if it costs me freedom.
I don't want visibility if it quietly teaches my heart to look sideways instead of upward.
Jesus asks a question that feels especially relevant in public spaces:
How can you believe when you receive glory from one another and do not seek the glory that comes from God alone?
That question doesn't tell me to hide.
It tells me to orient.
I don't want other people—whether readers, customers, followers, or critics—to become the ones who assign my worth. They can appreciate what I offer. They can choose to engage or not. But they cannot crown me, and they cannot diminish me.
I don't want to sit on a throne built by opinions.
I've watched what happens when people do.
Admiration slowly becomes elevation.
Elevation becomes expectation.
Expectation becomes pressure.
And pressure eventually breaks what was never meant to carry it.

.

No human was designed to bear the weight of being
admired as ultimate. Not even quietly. Not even
unintentionally.
That's why Paul's words steady me:
Do nothing from selfish ambition or conceit, but in
humility count others more significant than yourselves.
That isn't about shrinking my work or my voice.
It's about refusing distortion.
When my eyes are fixed on God, I can offer what I make
freely—without needing it to prove me.
I can receive encouragement without becoming dependent
on it.
I can handle success without being inflated.
And I can handle disappointment without being undone.
Whatever I do, I want to do it wholeheartedly—as unto the
Lord, not unto people.
Because when God remains the only One on the throne,
everything else finds its proper place.
Exposure becomes a tool, not a trap.
Success becomes stewardship, not identity.
And failure becomes feedback, not condemnation.
I don't want my value to rise and fall with algorithms,
opinions, or outcomes.
I want my life anchored in the quiet, unshakable approval
of God.
If He is pleased, I can move forward freely.
If He redirects, I can rest securely.
And if He blesses what I'm building, I can receive it
without bowing to it
That is the life I want to live—
visible, but grounded.
productive, but free.
successful, but un-enthroned.

## A Reflective Question

Where am I allowing visibility, success, or approval to subtly shape my sense of worth—and what would it look like to re-anchor my value fully in God's eyes instead?

## A Lap Prayer

God...
I'm right here again—close, honest, unguarded.
You know why I'm stepping into these spaces.
You know the practical reasons.
You know the hopes—and the risks.
I don't want to trade freedom for approval.
I don't want ease if it costs me clarity.
I don't want success if it slowly moves You off the throne.
Help me hold exposure loosely.
Help me receive affirmation without depending on it.
Help me build wisely without bowing to outcomes.
Keep my eyes on You.
Keep my heart anchored in Your pleasure.
And if You bless what I'm building, help me receive it with humility and open hands.
I want to live seen—but not owned.
Known—but not defined.
Successful—but surrendered.
You alone get the throne.
I'm content at Your feet.
Amen.

# Invitation Twenty-Eight: Obedience Without an Audience

Lately, my heart has been settling into a quieter question.
What does obedience look like when no one is watching?
Not obedience that earns approval.
Not obedience that gets noticed.
Not obedience that builds momentum or platform.
But obedience that happens unseen—
because God asked,
because I love Him,
because I trust Him.
Jesus spoke directly to this kind of obedience.
In Matthew 6, He warns against practicing righteousness in
order to be seen by others. He talks about giving, praying,
and living faithfully—not as public displays, but as private
acts of devotion. Again and again, He says the same
phrase:
"Your Father, who sees in secret..."
There is something deeply comforting—and deeply
clarifying—about that.
God sees.
Even when no one else does.
Especially when no one else does.
And yet, Jesus also makes something else very clear:
obedience in secret is not meant to be a strategy to earn
reward. It's meant to flow from love.
That distinction matters.
I think about my grandchildren helping me(they call me
Nawny) in the garden or around the house. There are
moments when they see something that needs doing and
jump in without being asked—pulling weeds, carrying
tools, handing me something I need, carrying groceries.
And when they do that, it blesses my heart in a way I can't
fully explain.

And when they help me simply because they know it delights my heart—because they love me—it makes me want to bless them in return. Sometimes I do. Sometimes I give them a treat, or a little money, or something special as a thank you.

But if they were to help me for the reward—if it became an exchange—that sweetness would be lost. It would still be helpful, but it wouldn't be the same. It wouldn't be relational. It wouldn't be love.

Jesus is inviting us into that same posture with the Father. In Matthew 6:3–4, He says that when we give, we shouldn't even let our left hand know what our right hand is doing—so that our giving remains free from self-consciousness and self-promotion. And in Matthew 6:6, He tells us to pray in private, with the door shut, not to be seen by others, but to be with the Father.

Not for show.

Not for applause.

Not for affirmation.

Just relationship.

Because God is not interested in managing our image—He is interested in shaping our hearts.

Obedience offered quietly does something deep in me. It strips away performance. It exposes motive. It asks me who I'm really doing this for.

And if I'm honest, there is still something in me that wants to be known. Wants to be acknowledged. Wants a witness.

But God keeps drawing me back and whispering something steadier:
You don't need to be known by the world if you are fully known by Me.
There is freedom in that.
Because when obedience is aimed at people, it becomes fragile. It bends with opinion. It negotiates with comfort. It weakens under pressure.
But when obedience is aimed at God alone, it becomes grounded. Humble. Whole.
I don't want to obey so that God will reward me.
I want to obey because I can't resist His company.
Because I love being near Him.
Because I love working alongside Him.
Because pleasing His heart somehow, mysteriously, ends up pleasing mine more deeply than anything else ever could.
And I don't want the praise of people at the expense of intimacy with God
I don't want my faith to become a public performance while my private life grows thin.
So I'm learning to choose obedience that no one may ever see.
Faithfulness that won't be announced.
Righteousness that doesn't need to be declared.
I'm learning to trust that God sees—and that His seeing is enough.
Because when humility governs my obedience, and love is the motive, obedience becomes a joy instead of a burden.
And in those quiet places—
those unseen moments—
I find that God is already there, smiling, pleased, inviting me closer.

## A Reflective Question

Where might I be tempted to seek recognition for my
faithfulness—and what would it look like to choose
obedience there simply because it delights God's heart?

## A Conversational Lap Prayer

Hey, God...
It's just me and You right now.
I don't want to impress anyone.
I don't want to keep score.
I don't want to obey just so I'll get something back.
I want to do what pleases You because I love You.
Because I love being close to You.
Because I love knowing it makes Your heart glad.
Help me notice where I'm tempted to be seen.
Gently pull me back when my motives drift.
Teach me to love the quiet obedience—the kind that only
You and I know about.
Thank You for seeing me.
Thank You for delighting in my willingness.
Thank You for letting me work beside You, not as a
transaction, but as a relationship.
I don't need applause.
I just want You.
Amen

# Invitation Twenty-Nine: Anchored in the Storm

There's a bird feeder on my window that God keeps using
to teach me about Himself.
It's been there since April—clear, sturdy, filled with really
good seed. Not the cheap stuff. The kind songbirds can't
resist. It hangs right on the glass, close enough that I can sit
inside and watch them once they stop being startled by my
presence.
And for months—spring, summer, fall—not a single bird
touched it.
The feeder stayed full. The seed stayed ready. But the birds
had plenty elsewhere. The fields were generous. The plants
were heavy with seed. Life was easy.
Then winter came.
And then an ice storm.
Everything outside was sealed in glass—branches, ground,
leaves. Beautiful, but impossible. The birds couldn't get to
what had always sustained them. And suddenly, that feeder
became visible.
They came.
Tentative at first. Then confident. Then constant. Once
they discovered nourishment that didn't require frantic
searching—once they realized there was a steady place,
right there—they kept returning.
Even when the ice melted.
Even when the sun came out.
Even when things looked easier again.
Now, as snow falls and the natural food sources are hidden,
they know exactly where to go.
And it's impossible not to see myself in them.
God has always been there.

Scripture tells me again and again that He is my refuge.
My strength. A very present help in trouble. I don't have to
beg Him to show up in storms—He's already there. I don't
have to chase Him down or wonder where He is. I don't
have to fear being abandoned when the wind picks up.
He's right there.
Like that feeder on the window—unchanging, steady, full
—whether I notice Him or not.
Psalm 46 tells me He is present.
Isaiah 41 reminds me not to fear, because He is with me.
Psalm 139 says that even in the farthest reaches, even in
the depths, His hand still holds me.
Storms don't mean His absence.
They often mean my attention is finally focused.
And God doesn't promise a storm-free life. He never tells
me to expect calm seas all the time. But He does tell me
where to go when the waves rise.
Philippians reminds me not to be anxious—but to bring
everything to Him. Not with panic. Not with striving. But
with trust. And when I do, His peace guards my heart and
my mind. That peace doesn't erase the storm—it anchors
me inside it.
I'm learning to see storms not as interruptions, but as
invitations.
Every storm carries the potential to deepen my faith.
Every storm can drive me closer to the Father.
Every storm can strip away what has been veiling His
image in me.

Growth rarely happens in comfort. It happens when I stop staring at the waves and lift my eyes to His face—when I remember what He has already done, how He has already been faithful, how He has already carried me through before.
Sometimes He stills the storm.
Sometimes He stills me.
Psalm 107 says He makes the storm calm. And even when He doesn't quiet it right away, His grace remains sufficient.
His power shows up most clearly when I'm weak.
The victory is already won.
He has already overcome the world.
I'm just walking it out—held, protected, led.
So this is my desire—not to avoid storms, but to be anchored through them.
To remember that God is not activated by my crisis—He is constant.
To lean into His promises instead of reacting to fear.
To let storms refine me until what people see more clearly is Christ.
I don't want to treat God like a last resort when life freezes over.
I want to stay close—rooted in His Word, anchored in His presence—so that when storms come, I already know where my nourishment is.
Because He is my refuge.
He is my strength.
And He is already here.

## A Reflective Question

When storms arise, do I scramble for peace—or do I return
to the place I already know will nourish and steady me?

## A Quiet, Conversational Prayer

God...
I see how quickly storms sharpen my focus.
Thank You for never leaving—
not when things feel calm,
and not when everything is shaking.
Help me remember that You are not hiding from me in
hard seasons.
You're right here.
Waiting.
Steady.
Full.
Teach me to come to You first—not out of panic, but out of
trust.
To curl up close instead of scanning the horizon for
escape.
To look into Your eyes instead of staring at the waves.
If storms are going to come—and I know they will—
let them shape me.
Strip away what doesn't belong.
Reveal more of You in me.
I don't need a life without storms.
I just need You.
And I know You're already here.
Amen

# Invitation Thirty: Honestly Speaking — Remain

Honestly speaking...
this isn't the end of anything.
It's the place where I finally stop pretending I'm farther
along than I am.
It's where I stop bracing myself.
It's where I stop managing the image and simply remain.
When I look back over these invitations—waiting,
surrender, grief, obedience, joy, truth, leaven, aroma,
unseen faithfulness, storms, trust—I don't see a system to
maintain.
I see a relationship that has been deepening.
And somewhere along the way, without fanfare, something
else has happened.
I've begun to take off the mask.
Not all at once.
Not dramatically.
But honestly.
The mask I put on to be strong.
The mask I put on to be acceptable.
The mask I put on because at one point it felt necessary for
survival.
Honestly speaking, I understand now why I wore it.
But I also understand why I don't need it anymore.
Because the longer I remain with Him—
the more I look into His eyes instead of scanning for
danger—
the more I realize He has never been fooled by the mask
and never threatened by what's underneath it.
He sees all of me.
The beautiful parts.
The broken parts.
The places I'm proud of.
The places I'd rather hide.

And still—He stays.
He doesn't recoil from the ugly places.
He doesn't shame the unfinished ones.
He doesn't withdraw when I stop performing.
Instead, He leans in.
Because He knows those places are not evidence of failure
—
they're invitations for His hands to work.
Like a potter with clay, He doesn't discard what's
misshapen.
He presses.
He reshapes.
He softens what's hardened.
He forms something stunning out of what once felt
unpresentable.
Honestly speaking, remaining with Him has changed what
honesty even means to me.
It's no longer confession driven by fear.
It's conversation rooted in trust.
I don't have to curate myself before I come to Him.
I don't have to clean up first.
I don't have to hide what I'm still becoming.
I just come.
And that has become the invitation beneath every other
invitation in this book.
Remain.
Stay.
Tell the truth.
Not the polished truth.
The real one.
Because the work He's doing in me doesn't require a mask
—
it requires presence.
This life with God isn't built on intensity.
It's built on constancy.

Not dramatic breakthroughs, but daily returning.
Not flawless obedience, but honest surrender.
Not being seen, but being known.
And I want that to be the rhythm of my life.
To go to Him first—before fear, before fixing, before defending.
To stay rooted when storms come instead of scrambling for control.
To let joy remain even when happiness wavers.
To tend what is alive in me with care.
To carry His aroma quietly into every room.
To be content being unseen, as long as I am fully known by Him.
Honestly speaking, I don't want these invitations to be something I read and move past.
I want them to become how I live.
I want my reflex to be honesty.
My instinct to be trust.
My anchor to be His presence.
And when I forget—and I will—
I don't have to start over.
I just return.
This isn't a finish line.
It's a lifelong invitation:
Remain.
Abide.
Stay uncovered.Let Him do the work.
Let Him carry the weight.
Let Him complete what He began.
And trust—deeply, quietly, steadily—
that His hands are gentle,
His intentions are good,
and His work in me is beautiful
even while it's unfinished.

**A Question to Carry Forward**

Honestly speaking, what mask am I still tempted to wear—
and what might change if I trusted God enough to remain
fully seen?

**A Closing, Quiet Prayer**

God...
Honestly speaking, it's just me here.
No polishing.
No proving.
No mask.
Thank You for never needing one from me.
Thank You for seeing beauty even where I only see mess.
Thank You for staying close enough to do the work I can't.
Teach me how to remain—
open, honest, and unguarded.
Not because I'm brave,
but because You are kind.
I trust Your hands.
I trust Your heart.
I trust the work You're doing in me.
I'm here.
I'm staying.
Amen